CANADIAN GRAMMAR SPECTRUM

REFERENCE AND PRACTICE

Norman Coe

OXFORD
UNIVERSITY PRESS

OXFORD
UNIVERSITY PRESS

Oxford University Press is a department of the University of Oxford.
It furthers the University's objective of excellence in research, scholarship, and education by publishing worldwide.
Oxford is a registered trade mark of Oxford University Press in the UK and in certain other countries.

Published in Canada by
Oxford University Press
8 Sampson Mews, Suite 204,
Don Mills, Ontario M3C 0H5 Canada

www.oupcanada.com

Copyright © Oxford University Press Canada 2012
The moral rights of the author have been asserted
Database right Oxford University Press (maker)

First Edition Published in 2012

Oxford Practice Grammar was originally published in 2006. This edition is published by arrangement with
Oxford University Press, Great Clarendon Street, Oxford OX2 6DP, United Kingdom.

Library and Archives Canada Cataloguing in Publication

Coe, Norman
Canadian grammar spectrum 3 : reference and practice / Norman Coe.

Includes index.
Previously published as part of: Coe, Norman.
Oxford practice grammar.
Basic, 2006.
ISBN 978-0-19-544706-4

1. English language—Grammar—Problems, exercises, etc.
2. English language—Textbooks for second language learners.
I. Coe, Norman. Oxford practice grammar. Basic. II. Title.

PE1128.C56 2011   428.2'4   C2011-900738-X

Oxford University Press is committed to our environment.
This book is printed on Forest Stewardship Council® certified paper,
harvested from a responsibly managed forest.

MIX
Paper from
responsible sources
FSC® C004071

Printed and bound in Canada.

7   8   9   —   20   19   18

Contents

	page
Introduction	1

Verbs and tenses

Simple Present	2
Present Progressive	4
Simple Present or Present Progressive	6
Simple Past	8
Simple Past or Past Progressive	10
Used to	12
Present Perfect	14
Simple Past or Present Perfect	16
Present Perfect or Present Perfect Progressive	18
Past Perfect	20
Will or **be going to**	22
Future	24
Second Conditional (Unreal Conditional)	26
Third Conditional (Past Conditional)	28
Make, do, have, get	30
Phrasal verbs (1): meanings and types	32
Phrasal verbs (2): separability	34

Modals and other verbs

Must, can't, may, might, could	36
Must/have to, must not/don't have to	38
Need, doesn't need, didn't need to	40
Should, ought to, had better	42
Had to …, should have …	44

Passive

Passive sentences (1)	46
Passive sentences (2)	48
Have something done	50

Infinitives and –ing forms

Verb + **to** or verb + **-ing**	52
Purpose: for …ing	54
Verb + object (+ **to**) + infinitive	56

Questions

What … like?	58

Reported speech

Reported speech (1)   60
Reported speech (2)   62
Reported questions   64

Articles

Articles: a/an, the, or no article   66

There and *it*

There or it/they   68

Adjectives and adverbs

So and such   70
Adjective + preposition   72
Position of adverbs in a sentence   74

Prepositions

Prepositions of place and movement   76
Other uses of prepositions   78

Building sentences

Relative clauses (1)   80
Relative clauses (2)   82
Since, as, for   84
Although, while, however, despite, etc.   86
Because, in case, so, so that   88

Review test

                                                                90

Appendices

Appendix 1: Nouns   94
Appendix 2: Regular verbs   95
Appendix 3: Irregular verbs   96
Appendix 4: Adjectives and adverbs   97

Answer key

                                                                98

Index

                                                               106

Introduction

Canadian Grammar Spectrum is a series of books, each written at the appropriate level for you at each stage in your study of English. The series is intended for your use either in a classroom or when working independently on your own time.

The books are divided into two-page units, each of which covers an important grammar topic. Each unit starts with an explanation of the grammar and is followed by a set of practice exercises. A test at the end of each book gives the opportunity for more practice and enables you to assess how much you have learned. Answers to the exercises and the tests are provided at the back of the book.

You may want to choose the order in which you study the grammar topics, perhaps going first to those which are giving you problems. (Topics are listed in the Contents page at the front of each book and in the Index at the back.) Alternatively, you may choose to start at the beginning of each book and work through to the end.

Key to symbols

The symbol / (oblique stroke) between two words means that either word is possible. *We write **does** before **he/she/it*** means that *We write **does** before **he***, *We write **does** before **she*** and *We write **does** before **it*** are all possible. In exercise questions, this symbol is also used to separate words or phrases which are possible answers.

Parentheses ( ) around a word or phrase in the middle of a sentence mean that it can be left out. *She said (that) she lived in a small apartment* means that there are two possible sentences: *She said that she lived in a small apartment* and *She said she lived in a small apartment*.

The symbol ~ means that there is a change of speaker. In the example *When did Jane go to India? ~ In June*, the question and answer are spoken by different people.

The symbol ▶ in an exercise indicates that a sample answer is given.

Simple Present

1 We use the Simple Present:
  ▶ to talk about feelings and opinions:

> I **like** pop music. I **don't like** classical music.
> She **loves** lacrosse!
> Philip **wants** a new car.
> I **don't want** a cup of coffee, thanks.
> He **feels** sick.

  ▶ to talk about thoughts:

> I **don't think** she likes her new job.
> I **don't know** the answer.
> He **doesn't understand** me.

2 We form Simple Present questions like this:

QUESTIONS			
Singular	Do	I/you	know?
	Does	he/she/it	
Plural	Do	we	
	Do	you	know?
	Do	they	

Note that we put **do** before **I/you/we/they**:
> *Do you* **speak** *Spanish?*
> *Do you* **work** *downtown?*
> *Do they* **know** *the answer?*

We put **does** before **he/she/it**:
> *Does he* **walk** *to work?*
> *Does Steve* **enjoy** *his job?*
> *Does she* **play** *the piano?*

Note that we say:
> *Does he* **walk**? (NOT ~~Does he walks?~~)

Practice

A Write the words from the box in the correct form. Use the Simple Present. Use each verb once.

ride	see	have	not taste	want	~~enjoy~~	drink	not like

  ▶ He wants to work as a librarian, because he *enjoys* .... books.
  1 Wow! You can .... the Northern Lights from here.
  2 They love their dog, but they .... cats.
  3 Is there sugar in this? I .... any.
  4 Barry .... his snowmobile almost every day in the winter.
  5 Let's invite Marcel to go with us. Do you .... his number?
  6 My mom .... a cup of coffee before work every morning.
  7 We .... to see your new apartment this weekend.

B Write sentences about Monique. (✓ = likes, ✓✓ = loves, ✗ = does not like, ✗✗ = hates)

  ▶ (coffee ✗)   *She doesn't like coffee.* ....
  ▶ (swimming ✓)   *She likes swimming.* ....
  1 (her job ✓✓)   She ....
  2 (cold weather ✗✗)   She ....
  3 (reading ✓)   ....
  4 (basketball ✗✗)   ....
  5 (mushrooms ✗)   ....
  6 (learning languages ✓✓) ....

C This is an interview with Chris Rampaul about himself and his brother, Ken. Write the questions, using the ideas from the box.

have any children	~~drink a lot of pop~~	play cards	~~work at a car factory~~
exercise often	live in Saskatchewan	play soccer	enjoy public speaking
like sailing	like travelling	live in an apartment	like scary movies
have a car	speak any foreign languages		

QUESTIONS

▶ *Do you work at a car factory* .... ?
▶ *Does Ken drink a lot of pop* .... ?
1 .... ?
2 .... ?
3 .... ?
4 .... ?
5 .... ?
6 .... ?
7 .... ?
8 .... ?
9 .... ?
10 .... ?
11 .... ?
12 .... ?

ANSWERS

~ No, I work in a restaurant.
~ Yes, he drinks some every day.
~ Yes, I sail very often in the summer.
~ Yes, I like to play euchre.
~ No, he lives in Manitoba.
~ Yes, I have a small convertible.
~ No, he doesn't play soccer.
~ Yes, I can speak Italian and Spanish.
~ No, he doesn't have any children.
~ No, I prefer comedies.
~ Yes, he goes to the gym very often.
~ No, I hate speaking to large groups.
~ Yes, I live in an apartment on Beech Street.
~ No, he likes to stay at home.

D You are on vacation, and you are at a Tourist Information Centre. Ask questions using the table below.

A	B	C
Do	~~you~~	speak English?
Does	the volcano	ever get cooler?
	the bus	become dangerous at night?
	the tour guides	~~sell maps of the city?~~
	that restaurant	require reservations?
	the temperature	erupt often?
	the locals	have a favourite bar?
	this area	stop in front of my hotel?

▶ *Do you sell maps of the city?* ....
1 .... the volcano ....
2 ....
3 ....
4 ....
5 ....
6 ....
7 ....

Present Progressive

1 Look at these questions:
>*Are you **enjoying** that drink, Ann?*
>*Is he **watching** TV at the moment?*
>*Are they **working** hard?*

2 We form Present Progressive questions like this:

QUESTIONS		
Singular	Am I	
	Are you	} winning?
	Is she/he/it	
Plural	Are we	
	Are you	} winning?
	Are they	

3 Here are two common Present Progressive questions. They both mean "How are you?":
>*How's it **going**?*
>*How **are** you **doing**?*

4 We do not usually use the Present Progressive to talk about opinions or thoughts:
>*I **like** tennis. I **know** your sister.* (NOT ~~I'm liking tennis. I'm knowing your sister.~~)

We do not usually use these verbs in the Present Progressive:

like	know	hate
love	understand	believe
mean	remember	want

5 **think** and **have**:
▶ we cannot use **think** in the Present Progressive to express opinions:
>*I **think** he's nice.* (NOT ~~I'm thinking he's nice.~~)

▶ we can use **think** in the Present Progressive to talk about an action:
>*She's **thinking** about the movie.*

▶ we cannot use **have** in the Present Progressive to talk about possessions:
>*I **have** a ticket.* (NOT ~~I am having a ticket.~~)

▶ we can use it to talk about actions:
>*I'm **having** breakfast. He's **having** fun.*

Practice

A Write questions by putting the words in parentheses ( ) in the correct order.

▶ (enjoying – your work – you – are – ?)   <u>Are you enjoying your work?</u>

1 (making cookies – are – they – ?)

2 (is – getting angry – your boss – ?)

3 (playing well – am – I – ?)

4 (your brother – is – leaving – ?)

5 (they – are – singing – in the concert – ?)

6 (we – are – moving – ?)

7 (is – up north – he – skiing – ?)

8 (is – visiting her cousin – she – ?)

9 (having – are – dinner with Scott – we – ?)

10 (speaking clearly – I – am – ?)

B Write questions and answers. Use the Present Progressive.

QUESTIONS

ANSWERS

▶ (she/work/in Peru this year?)
Is she working in Peru this year?

~ (No, she/study/in Mexico)
~ No, she's studying in Mexico.

1 (they/speak/Japanese?)
....

~ (No, they/speak/Korean)
~
....

2 (you/read/right now?)
....

~ (Yes, I/read/great novel)
~
....

3 (Shea/run/in this blizzard?)
....

~ (No, he/nap/on the couch)
~
....

4 (you/write/email to Igor?)
....

~ (Yes, I/tell/him about my vacation)
~
....

5 (Claudia/dance/at the festival today?)
....

~ (No, she/work/at the information booth)
~
....

C Put a check (✓) next to a correct sentence, and an X (✗) next to an incorrect sentence.

▶ She's liking pop music. ✗
▶ He's learning French. ✓
1 They're wanting to leave now.
2 I'm having a great time.
3 Your coffee is getting cold.
4 Paulo is believing everything he hears.
5 My dad is worrying about the weather.

6 She's walking through the field.
7 I am meaning to tell him the story.
8 We're painting the barn.
9 Yvonne is liking to ride horses.
10 He's knowing my history teacher.

D Complete this conversation. Use the verbs in parentheses ( ) in the Present Progressive.

Emil: Hi, Jenna. What's up?

Jenna: (▶) I'm going............ (I/go) to my weekly cooking class.

Emil: That's great! I didn't know you liked to cook. (1)....................... (you/enjoy)
          the classes?

Jenna: Of course. (2)....................... (I/learn) a lot and, best of all,
          (3)....................... (I/eat) lots of wonderful food.

Emil: And I'm sure (4)....................... (you/meet) other people who love to cook!
          What (5)....................... (you/make) this week?

Jenna: Our instructor (6)....................... (teach) us how to make perfect Peking duck.
          (7)....................... (I/look) forward to it! What (8)....................... (you/do)
          tonight?

Emil: Well, Jimmy and I (9)....................... (go) to a basketball game. Then
          (10)....................... (we/go) to the blues bar on Queen Street where Jimmy's
          brother (11)....................... (play) the saxophone.

Simple Present or Present Progressive

Compare the Simple Present and the Present Progressive:

1 We use the Simple Present to talk about facts (things which are true at any time):

*Anna **speaks** good Mandarin.*
*Journalists **write** newspaper articles.*
*I **come** from Norway. (= I am Norwegian).*

We use the Present Progressive to talk about actions in progress at the time of speaking:

*Anna's busy. She's **speaking** on the phone.*
*What **are** you **writing**? ~ A letter to Jane.*
*Look! The bus **is coming**.*

2 We use the Simple Present for situations that exist over a long time, and for actions that are repeated (e.g. people's habits, or events on a timetable):

*Mike **works** for an advertising company.*
*He **lives** in Vancouver. (= His home is in Vancouver.)*

We use the Present Progressive for things that continue for a limited period of time around now (e.g. vacations, visits, temporary jobs, school or university courses):

*John **is working** in the US for six months.*
*He's **living** in New York.*

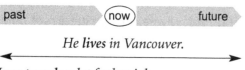

*He **lives** in Vancouver.*

*Jane **travels** a lot for her job.*
*I **play** a lot of sports.*

We can use words like **usually, often, every**:

*We **usually go** out to dinner on weekends.*
*I **often go** to baseball games on Sundays.*
*The buses **leave every** hour.*

*He's **living** in New York.*

*Jane's **travelling** around Europe for a month.*
*I'm **doing** a one-year course in tourism.*
*We're **painting** the apartment.*

3 We use the Simple Present with thinking and feeling verbs (e.g. **know, forget, notice, understand, recognize, remember, like, love, hate, want, prefer, need**):

*I **don't know** which train to catch.*

We do not usually use the Present Progressive with thinking and feeling verbs:

NOT ~~I'm knowing someone who lives in Venice.~~

4 We use **have** in the Simple Present to talk about possession:

*I **have** a new car.*

We use **think** in the Simple Present to express opinions:

*I **think** she's interesting.*

We use **have** and **think** in the Present Progressive to talk about actions:

*I'm **having** fun.*
*He can't come, he's **having** dinner at the moment.*
*I am **thinking** about my work.*

Practice

A **Complete the sentences with the Simple Present (*I do*) or the Present Progressive (*I am doing*).**

▶ I .....leave..... (leave) home at seven o'clock every morning.

1 I .... (look) for a book about Aboriginal history, but I can't .... (find) the one I want.

2 She .... (paint) a portrait of Maxine.

3 Francisco .... (want) a new car but he doesn't .... (have) enough money.

4 I .... (call) her right now. Would you like to speak to her?
5 He .... (have) trouble with his math homework.
6 Can everyone .... (see) the statue from here?
7 Trent .... (try) to jump over the fence.
8 The bus usually .... (stop) right here. Why .... (it/drive) past us?
9 Kyle .... (invite) 70 people to his birthday party.
10 You .... (look) exhausted. You .... (work) too hard this week.

B **This is Grace's first letter in English to Jerome. There are some mistakes in it. Cross out the incorrect verb forms and write in the correct form. Put a check (✓) if the form of the verb is correct.**

Dear Jerome,

I am staying (▶) ✓ .... in an apartment in Vancouver. This city is being (▶) is .... on the west coast of Canada. Many interesting people live (1) .... here. Sometimes I meet (2) .... artists and musicians. When I am having (3) .... time, I talk to them about their work. People here are being (4) .... very friendly.

There are also mountains nearby, and I ski (5) .... whenever I can. I had never skied before coming to Canada, but I take (6) .... lessons right now and I am learning (7) .... quickly. Are you liking (8) .... to ski?

I love (9) .... Vancouver, but I miss everyone back home. I am wishing (10) .... you could all come here!

Take care,
Grace

C **Write the sentences using the Simple Present or the Present Progressive.**

▶ (Usually she/work/at the office, but this week she/work/at home)
   Usually she works at the office, but this week she's working at home.

1 (I/smell/something spicy. Dad must/make/chili)
   ....

2 (Wendy/have/an appointment this afternoon)
   ....

3 (He/work/late again because he/have/an important meeting to prepare for)
   ....

4 (You/speak/very loudly right now. Is your hearing okay?)
   ....

5 (We/build/a snowman. You should come and help us!)
   ....

6 (She/walk/to work every morning)
   ....

7 (I/watch/my favourite TV show right now)
   ....

8 (The wind/blow/the leaves everywhere)
   ....

Simple Past

1 We form the Simple Past of regular verbs by adding **-ed** to the verb:

> walk → walked   watch → watched
> open → opened   ask → asked

There are some exceptions:

▶ verbs ending with **-e**:

> **+ -d:**   live → lived   like → liked

▶ verbs ending with a consonant and **-y**:

> **-y → -ied:**   apply → applied
>   try → tried

▶ most verbs ending with one vowel and one consonant:

> **-p → -pped:**   stop → stopped
>   plan → planned

(For more details on the form of the Simple Past, see Appendix 2, page 95.)

2 Many verbs have an irregular Simple Past form:

> do → did   have → had
> take → took   buy → bought
> come → came   stand → stood
> find → found   ring → rang
> go → went   say → said

(For more details, see Appendix 3, page 96.)

3 We form the negative with **didn't** and the infinitive (e.g. **do, take, understand**):
> I **didn't understand.** (NOT ~~didn't understood~~)

We form questions with **did** and the infinitive (e.g. **watch**):
> **Did** you **watch** the movie?

4 We use the Simple Past to talk about an action or situation in the past which is finished. We often say when it happened (e.g. **yesterday, last night**):
> Chris **called** me **yesterday.** He **wanted** to ask me something.
> **Did** you **enjoy** the concert **last night**?

5 We can use the Simple Past with **for** to talk about something that continued for a period of time, and ended in the past:
> I **lived** in Rome **for two years.** Then I went to work in Japan.

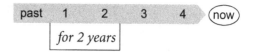

Practice

A Put a check (✓) next to the correct forms of the Simple Past, and cross out those which are incorrect. You can look at Appendix 3, page 96, before you do the exercise.

~~writed~~	falled	cooked	readed	fell	won
loved ✓	shooted	buyed	threw	runned	woke
bought	read	shaked	write	stealed	bitted
eated	ran	waked	winned	drew	finded
passed	swimmed	drawed	shot	maked	shook
found	made	bit	throwed	swam	stole

B Complete the sentences using the Simple Past form and the words in parentheses ( ).

► We _went_ .... (go) skiing last weekend.
1 She .... (make) a beautiful dress.
2 I .... (see) my best friend yesterday, and we .... (play) baseball together.
3 The chief .... (say) something, but the people .... (not/hear) him.
4 My little sister .... (hit) me, but then she .... (say) sorry.
5 I .... (call) my dad and .... (talk) to him about the party.
6 A: .... (you/read) the book?
   B: Yes! I .... (start) it on Tuesday, and I .... (finish) yesterday.
7 I .... (run) 10 kilometres this morning, then I .... (eat) a big breakfast.
8 A: .... (you/enjoy) the game?
   B: Yes. Our team .... (play) well, and we .... (win).

C Write sentences using the correct form of the Simple Past.

► (Who/eat/the last crepe?) _Who ate the last crepe?_ ....
1 (When/Caroline/finish/university?)
   ....
2 (She/go/to a movie last night, but she/not/like it)
   ....
3 (you/visit/Margaret last week?)
   ....
4 (Jeff/start/a new business last month, and he/hire/six employees)
   ....
5 (I/see/Ashad the other day, but I/not/recognize/him)
   ....
6 (Maddie/feel/sick yesterday, so she/go/to the doctor)
   ....

D It's the beginning of a new semester at university. Two students, Nick and Eric, are talking about their summer vacation. Complete their conversation using the correct Simple Past form of the words in parentheses ( ).

Nick: What (►) _did you do_ .... (you/do) in the summer?
Eric: I (1)...................... (take) a trip around Europe by train.
Nick: (2)...................... (you/go) on your own, or with some friends?
Eric: A couple of friends (3)...................... (come) with me.
Nick: How many countries (4)...................... (you/visit)?
Eric: I (5)...................... (go) to six or seven countries. I (6)...................... (have)
       a great time, and I really (7)...................... (love) all of them.
Nick: Which one (8)...................... (you/like) most?
Eric: Sweden, I think. I (9)...................... (enjoy) exploring the marvellous countryside
       and I (10)...................... (take) lots of photographs.
Nick: When (11)...................... (you/arrive) back home?
Eric: Last week. I'm still very tired.

Simple Past or Past Progressive

1 Compare the Simple Past and the Past Progressive:

SIMPLE PAST	PAST PROGRESSIVE
He *talked* to her last week.	He *was talking* to her when I saw him.
I *didn't talk* to her yesterday.	I *wasn't talking* to anyone, I was watching TV.
Did you *talk* to your sister?	*Were* you *talking* to her before I came?

2 We use the Simple Past to talk about a complete event in the past:

> Last Saturday morning, Jin **played** baseball in the park.

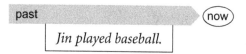

Here are some more examples:
> On Sunday I **made** a cake.
> It **rained** a lot on Saturday morning.

We use the Past Progressive to talk about an action that was in progress when something else happened:

> Last Saturday, Jin was playing baseball in the park when he saw Jane.

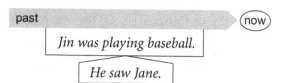

Here are some more examples:
> The phone rang while I **was making** a cake.
> It **was raining** when we left home.

3 We often use the Simple Past to talk about one event that followed another event:
> When Ann d'Angelo **finished** university, she **went** to work for a bank. She **left** the bank after five years, and **wrote** a book which ...

In a story we often use the Past Progressive to say what was in progress, when something happened:
> The sun **was shining**. People **were sitting** under the trees or **walking** around the park. Suddenly a car **drove** into the park ...

Practice

A Use the Simple Past and the Past Progressive to make sentences from the words in parentheses ( ).

▶ (The police/arrive/while/I/have/breakfast)
  The police arrived while I was having breakfast.

1 (The storm/start/while/they/drive/home)

2 (I/see/an accident/while/I/wait/for the bus)

3 (Mary/go/to several concerts/while/she/stay/in Calgary)

▶ (I/have/breakfast/when/the police/arrive)
  I was having breakfast when the police arrived.

4 (My father/cook/dinner/when/he/burn/his fingers)

5 (The soldiers/prepare/to leave/when/the bomb/explode)

B **Complete these passages using the Simple Past or the Past Progressive of the verbs in parentheses ( ).**

▶ Beethoven _wrote_......... (write) nine symphonies; he _was writing_.. (write) another symphony when he died.

1 Last Saturday Tom wanted to make two salads. He .... (make) the first one in five minutes. He .... (make) the second one when his guests .... (arrive), and they .... (help) him to finish it.

2 The artist Gaudi .... (design) several houses in Barcelona, Spain. Later he .... (start) work on a church. He .... (work) on the church when he .... (die).

3 Last month a bank robber .... (escape) while the police .... (take) him to prison. Later they .... (catch) him again, and this time they .... (lock) him up without any problem.

4 Pedro's hockey team was lucky last Saturday. After the first period they .... (lose), but in the end they .... (win) the game by four goals to two.

5 John Lennon .... (sing) and .... (play) on many records with the Beatles. After that he .... (record) several songs without the Beatles. He .... (prepare) a new record when Mark Chapman .... (shoot) him.

6 The evening was getting darker; the street lights .... (come) on. People .... (hurry) home after work. I .... (stand) in a line at the bus stop. Suddenly somebody .... (grab) my purse.

C **A police officer is interviewing Luisa Rivera about last Friday evening. Look at the pictures and complete the conversation. Use the Simple Past or the Past Progressive of the words in parentheses ( ).**

Police officer: What time (▶)_did you get_.......... (you/get) home from work?
Luisa: At about six o'clock.
Police officer: And what (1)....................... (you/do) after you got home?
Luisa: I read the newspaper.
Police officer: Did anything happen while (2)....................... (read) the paper?
Luisa: Yes, the phone (3)....................... (ring).
Police officer: What (4)....................... (you/do) when your husband came home?
Luisa: I was watching TV, and I (5)....................... (drink) a cup of coffee.
Police officer: Did you and your husband stay at home?
Luisa: No, I (6)....................... (drink) my coffee. Then I put on my raincoat, and we (7)....................... (go) out at seven o'clock.
Police officer: Why (8)....................... (you/put) your raincoat on?
Luisa: Because it (9)....................... (rain), of course.

Used to

1 We can use the Simple Present to talk about present situations or habits:

> ▶ situations:
> *My sister **works** as a translator.*
> *Andrew **lives** in Halifax.*

> ▶ habits:
> *Hilal usually **wears** jeans.*
> *I often **eat** a sandwich for lunch.*
> *Mike **doesn't smoke** anymore.*
> ***Does** Javier **drive** to work every day?*

2 Look at these sentences with the Simple Past:

> ▶ situation:
> *Portia **lived** in France for many years.*

> ▶ habit:
> *When I was young, I **ran** five kilometres every day.*

The verbs are in the Simple Past and the sentences are about past situations or habits.

3 Look at these sentences with **used to**:
> *Narmatha **used to live** in Vancouver.*
> *Many people **used to make** their own bread.*
> *My husband **used to work** at home.*

We use **used to** to talk about a past situation or habit that continued for months or years, and to emphasize that the situation today is different:
> *Narmatha doesn't live in Vancouver **now**.*
> ***Nowadays** people usually buy bread from a grocery store.*
> *My husband doesn't work at home **now**.*

Compare the Simple Past and **used to**:

> ▶ Simple Past:
> *When he was young, he **ran** five kilometres every day.* (He may or may not run five kilometres every day now.)
> ▶ used to:
> *When I was young, I **used to run** five kilometres every day.* (I don't run five kilometres every day now.)

We make negative sentences and questions with **did + use to**:
> *Sue **didn't use to like** black coffee.*
> *Saj **didn't use to smoke**.*
> ***Did** Alain **use to cycle** to school?*
> ***Did** your parents **use to read** to you?*

4 We do not use **use to** for present situations or habits; we use the Simple Present:
> *Ann **sings** in a band.* (NOT ~~Ann uses to sing in a band.~~)
> *Joe **doesn't cycle** to school.* (NOT ... ~~doesn't use to cycle~~...)

Practice

A **Look at this table of people who have changed what they eat or drink.**

name	Ann	Nik	Roberto	Pam	Adelfina	Susan
in the past	beef	coffee	white bread	tap water	frozen fruit	margarine
now	fish	tea	rye bread	bottled water	fresh fruit	butter

Now make sentences, as in the examples.

▶ Ann ..*used to eat*.... beef, but now she ..*eats fish*........ .

▶ Nik ..*drinks tea*...... now, but ..*he used to drink*.. coffee.

1 Roberto .... white bread, but now .... rye bread.

2 Pam .... tap water, but now .... bottled water.

3 Adelfina .... fresh fruit now, but .... frozen fruit.

4 Susan .... butter now, but .... margarine.

Now complete these questions.

▶ *Did Ann use to eat beef?* .... ~ Yes she did, but now she eats fish.

5 .... ~ Yes he did, but now he eats rye bread.

6 .... ~ Yes she did, but now she eats fresh fruit.

7 .... ~ Yes she did, but now she drinks bottled water.

Now complete these sentences.

▶ Ann *didn't use to eat* .... fish, but she does now.

▶ Nik drinks tea now, but he *didn't use to drink* .... it.

8 Susan .... butter, but she does now.

9 Adelfina eats fresh fruit now, but she .... it.

10 Pam drinks bottled water now, but she .... it.

B **Cross out all the sentences which are incorrect, as in the example.**

▶ When he was in grade school, Tony used to work very hard.

▶ ~~Last year Peter used to get a new bicycle for Christmas.~~

1 I didn't use to watch TV much, but I do now.

2 When he was a teenager, my father used to buy all The Tea Party's CDs.

3 Paul used to go the theatre almost every weekend.

4 Did Pamela used to go to the concert last night?

5 Vikram used to be really fit when he played a lot of volleyball.

6 Jean used to spend a lot of money on that new jacket he bought last week.

7 Kate didn't use to come to school yesterday because she was sick.

8 Jane used to play tennis a lot, but she doesn't have time now.

9 Did you use to go to the beach on vacation when you were a child?

10 We used to live in Mexico before we came here.

C **Complete the sentences to say what these people used to do and what they do now, as in the example.**

▶ Andrew/get up/seven o'clock/now/seven-thirty
Andrew used to get up at seven o'clock, but now he gets up at seven-thirty. ....

▶ I/swim/before work/now/after work
I used to swim before work, but now I swim after work. ....

1 Dan/play/violin/now/guitar
....

2 Anna/be/best friends/Angela/now/Celia
....

3 Marisa/take/dancing lessons/now/skating lessons
....

4 I/buy CDs/now/mp3s
....

5 Sun and Pierre/live/Montreal/now/Quebec City
....

6 David/drive/Yaris/now/Jaguar
....

Present Perfect

1 We form the Present Perfect using the present tense of have + a past participle:

> **POSITIVE**
>
> | FULL FORM | SHORT FORM |
> |---|---|
> | I/you **have arrived** | I've arrived |
> | he/she/it **has arrived** | he's arrived |
> | we/you/they **have arrived** | we've arrived |
>
> **NEGATIVE**
>
> | FULL FORM | SHORT FORM |
> |---|---|
> | I/you **have not arrived** | haven't |
> | he/she/it **has not arrived** | hasn't |
> | we/you/they **have not arrived** | haven't |
>
> **QUESTIONS**
>
> **Have** I/you **arrived?**
> **Has** he/she/it **arrived?**
> **Have** we/you/they **arrived?**

2 Regular past participles end in **-ed** or **-d**:

> played   travelled   arrived   washed

(For more regular past participles see Appendix 2, page 95.)

Many past participles are irregular:

> buy → bought   go → gone
> make → made

(For irregular past participles see Appendix 3, page 96.)

3 We use the Present Perfect:

> ▶ to talk about recent actions:

> At 6:00, Anne arrived home.
> At 6:01, we can say:
> *Anne **has arrived** home.*
>
> From 6:30 to 7:00, Anne ate her dinner.
> At 7:01, we can say:
> *She's **eaten** her dinner.*

> ▶ to talk about our lives:

> *I've **sailed** across the Atlantic.*
> *I've **seen** gorillas in Africa.*
> *I **haven't danced** the Flamenco.*

4 When we ask people about their lives, we often use **ever** (= at any time):
> *Have you **ever** been to Australia?*

When people talk about their lives, they sometimes use **never** (= not at any time):
> *I've **never** learned French.*

Note that **ever** and **never** come before the past participle.

Practice

A Use short forms (*I've seen, she's gone*) of the Present Perfect to write positive or negative sentences.

▶ (He/lose/his passport) — He's lost his passport.
▶ (She/not/see/her sister) — She hasn't seen her sister.
1 (We/visit/every province and territory) ....
2 (They/study/all weekend) ....
3 (I/not/sleep/well this week) ....
4 (They/go/to the city) ....
5 (She/not/see/that movie) ....
6 (You/find/a treasure) ....

Now use the Present Perfect to write questions.

▶ (you/see/John?)   Have you seen John? ....

7 (you/try/seal meat?) ....

8 (Sam/meet/Julia?) ....

9 (we/finish/studying?) ....

10 (they/be/honest with each other?) ....

B   Julio is talking about his travel plans. Write the correct past participles in the blanks.

I've (▶) worked .... (work) hard my whole life and I've never

(1)................ (take) a real vacation. My wife and I have

(2)................ (raise) four children and we have (3)................

(pay) for all of them to travel. I've (4)................ (hear) their

stories and I've (5)................ (see) their pictures and I've

always (6)................ (be) a little envious. Now that I've

(7)................ (retire), I've (8)................ (decide) to

travel the world as I've always (9)................ (want).

I've (10)................ (read) lots of travel guides,

I've (11)................ (plan) my route, and I've

(12)................ (buy) a new camera. Is there

anything I've (13)................ (forgot)?

C   Read the questions. If they refer to a recent event, put a check (✓). If they refer to someone's life, rewrite the sentence using *ever*.

▶ Have you had coffee?   ✓...

▶ Have you eaten elephant meat?   Have you ever eaten elephant meat? ....

1 Have you eaten breakfast? ....

2 Have you been to the opera? ....

3 Have you read the newspaper? ....

4 Have you been married? ....

5 Have you been to Mexico? ....

D   Now write true answers to the questions above, using either *this morning* or *never*.

▶ No, I haven't had coffee this morning. ....

▶ No, I've never eaten elephant meat. ....

1 ....

2 ....

3 ....

4 ....

5 ....

Simple Past or Present Perfect

Compare the Simple Past and the Present Perfect:

1 We use the Simple Past to talk about something that happened at a particular time in the past:

> *I **met** Vincenzo **at four o'clock.***
> *When **did** Jane go to India? ~ **In June.***
> *Martin **bought** a new car **last week.***

We use the Present Perfect to talk about the past, but not about when things happened:

> *I**'ve met** Vincenzo's girlfriend. She's nice.*
> ***Have** you ever **been** to India? ~ Yes, I have.*
> *I **have** never **bought** a new car.*

2 We use the Simple Past for situations or actions during a period of time that ENDED in the past:

> *I **worked** there **for two years.** I left last year.*

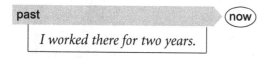

> I worked there for two years.

We use the Present Perfect for situations or actions during a period of time from the past to NOW:

> *He **has worked** here **for two years.***
> *(He still works here.)*

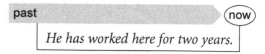

> He has worked here for two years.

> *We **lived** in that house **for a long time**; then we moved to this one.*
> *Our company **opened** two new stores **last summer.***

> *We**'ve lived** in this apartment **since we got married.** (We still live in it.)*
> *We opened two stores last summer. **Since then** (= since that time), we **have opened** two more.*

3 Notice how we often move from the Present Perfect to the Simple Past:

> Peter: *Have you ever **played** this game before?*
> Maria: *Yes, I **played** it once when I was in Alberta.*
> Peter: ***Did** you win?*
> Maria: *No, I **lost.***

Practice

A **Complete the conversation by choosing the correct form in parentheses ( ).**

Sarah: (▶) Have you ever been .... (Have you ever been/Did you ever go) to California?

Alvaro: Yes, (1).............................. (I've been/I went) there last year.

Sarah: (2).............................. (Have you liked/Did you like) it?

Alvaro: Yes, (3).............................. (I've enjoyed/I enjoyed) the trip a lot.

Sarah: What (4).............................. (have you done/did you do) there?

Alvaro: (5).............................. (I've visited/I visited) Hollywood, Disneyland, and San Francisco. (6).............................. (Have you been/Did you go) to California, Sarah?

Sarah: No, but (7).............................. (I've booked/I booked) a trip there. I've got my ticket and I'm going next week!

B Complete the dialogues using the Present Perfect (*I have seen*) or Simple Past (*I saw*).

A: I (▶) saw.......................... (see) Jack last night.
B: Oh really? I (1)............................... (not/see) him for months. How is he?

A: We (2)............................ (go) to the theatre last Saturday.
B: (3)............................... (you/enjoy) the play?
A: Yes, it (4)........................... (be) very good.

A: I (5)............................... (never/hear) of this band before. Are they popular in your country?
B: Yes, they are very popular. They (6)............................... (be) famous in my country for years.

A: What (7)............................... (you/do) last weekend?
B: I (8)............................... (stay) at home. I (9)............................... (need) a rest.

A: (10)............................... (you/ever/win) a competition?
B: Yes, I (11)............................... (win) a photo competition in 2010.

A: So, John is your best friend. (12)............................... (you/meet) him when you were in university?
B: Yes. We (13)............................... (be) friends for more than ten years.

C Complete this paragraph about the subway system in London, England, by writing the Present Perfect or Simple Past forms of the verbs in parentheses ( ).

THE LONDON UNDERGROUND

London (▶) has had............. (have) an underground train system since the
ninteenth century. The London Underground (1)........................ (start) in
1863, when Victorian engineers and workers (2)........................ (build) the
Metropolitan railway. This railway line (3)........................ (go) from
Paddington Station to Farringdon Street Station, and steam engines
(4)........................ (pull) the coaches. Eleven more lines
(5)........................ (open) since then. The world's first underground electric
railway (6)........................ (open) in 1890. This line (7)........................
(go) from the City of London to Stockwell in South London. The most modern
line is the Jubilee line, which (8)........................ (open) in 1979. Since the
London Underground (9)........................ (begin), many other cities, such as
New York and Toronto, (10)........................ (build) their own systems.

Present Perfect or Present Perfect Progressive

Compare the Present Perfect and Present Perfect Progressive:

1 We use the Present Perfect (**have painted**) to talk about a past activity that is now completed:

We've painted the rooms. (= The rooms are now painted.)
Anna has fixed her bike. (= She can ride it now.)

We use the Present Perfect Progressive (**have been painting**) to emphasize the activity itself, which may or may not be completed:

We've been painting the apartment. That's why it smells. We still have three rooms to paint.
Anna's hands are dirty because she's been fixing her bike.

2 We use the Present Perfect to ask and answer **How many?** and **How much?**:

A: *How many rooms have you painted?*
B: *We've painted three of them.*

We usually use the Present Perfect Progressive to ask **How long?**, and with **since** and **for**:
I have been travelling for six months.

A: *How long have you been waiting? Have you been waiting for a long time?*
B: *Yes, I've been waiting since two o'clock.*

3 Note that we usually use the Present Perfect (not the Progressive):

▶ to talk about short actions with **have, stop, break**, etc.
Tony has had an accident on his bike.

▶ with verbs of thinking (e.g. **know, decide, forget, notice**):
I'm sorry. I've forgotten your name.

▶ to talk about the last time that something happened:
I haven't eaten meat for two years. (= I last ate meat two years ago.)

Note that we can use the Present Perfect or Present Perfect Progressive with **work, teach**, and **live**, with no difference in meaning:
I have taught here for two years.
OR *I have been teaching here for two years.*

Practice

A Write out the sentences in parentheses ( ). Use the Present Perfect (e.g. *I have done*).

▶ He's late again. (How many times/he/arrive/late this month?)
How many times has he arrived late this month?

1 What a good week! (We/sell/much more than we expected.)
....

2 (How much money/you/spend/this week?)
....

3 (How many people/Junga/invite/to her party?)
....

Now use the Present Perfect Progressive (*I have been doing*).

4 It's still snowing. (It/snow/for hours.)
....

5 That noise is awful. (They/drill/holes in the wall all morning.)
....

6 Are you still here? (How long/you/sit/here?)
....

B Five friends have just finished some jobs. Look at the table.

	ACTIVITY	NOW
Neil	sweep the floors	he is sweating
Rachel	mow the lawn	she is tired
Paul	do the dishes	he has soft hands
Carol	peel the onions	she has red eyes
Erdem	defrost the fridge	he has cold hands

Complete the dialogues using this information. Use the Present Perfect or Present Perfect Progressive.

▶ Neil, why are you sweating?   ~ Because I *have been sweeping the floors.* ......

▶ Is the lawn finished?   ~ Yes, Rachel *has mowed the lawn.* ....

1 Paul, why are your hands so soft?   ~ Because I ....

2 Are the onions ready for the pan?   ~ Yes, Carol .... them.

3 Rachel, you look tired.   ~ Yes, I ....

4 Erdem, your hands are very cold.   ~ Yes, I ....

5 Are the floors clean?   ~ Yes, Neil .... them.

6 Why are your eyes red, Carol?   ~ Because I ....

7 Are the plates clean?   ~ Yes, Paul ....

8 Is the fridge all right now?   ~ Yes, Erdem ....

C Write the verbs in parentheses ( ) in the blanks in the correct form. Use the Present Perfect or Present Perfect Progressive.

▶ Ellen: Where are you and your family going to live?

    Liem: Well, we've *been talking* .... (talk) about that for weeks, but we haven't

           decided .... (decide) anything yet.

1 Tina: Excuse me. Have you .... (stand) in this line for a long time?

    Larry: Yes, I've .... (wait) for almost an hour.

2 Sara: Why are you crying?

    Joe: Because my brother has .... (have) an accident. He's

           .... (break) both his legs.

3 Susan: Excuse me. Has someone .... (forgot) this purse here?

    Dean: I don't know. I've .... (sit) here all afternoon, but I haven't

           .... (notice) it until now.

Past Perfect

1 We form the Past Perfect with **had** and the past participle of a verb (e.g. **started**, **taken**):

	FULL FORM	SHORT FORM
I/You/He/She/It/ We/They	**had started.**	**'d started.**

*I **had taken** it.* OR *I'd **taken** it.*
*They **had not started**.* OR *They **hadn't** started.*

2 Look at this:

A year ago:
Jenny is flying to Rome. She thinks, "I have never been on a plane before now."
Now:
*Jenny flew to Rome last year. She **had** never **been** on a plane before that.*

When we talk about an event or situation in past time we use the Simple Past (e.g. **flew**); if we talk about an event before that time, we use the Past Perfect (e.g. **had been**). Here is another example:

Last Saturday at the theatre:
Mary: *We don't need to line up because I've already bought the tickets.*
Now, talking about last Saturday:
Mary: *We didn't need to line up because I **had already bought** the tickets.*

Note that we can use **never** and **already** before the past participle (e.g. **been**, **bought**).

3 If we talk about a series of past events in order, we use the Simple Past:
    A: *I saw a beautiful bird in my backyard.*
    B: *I went to get my camera.*
    C: *The bird **flew** away.*
    D: *I returned with my camera.*

    past   A   B   C   D   (now)

We need the Past Perfect to make it clear that one of the events is not in order:
    D: *I returned with my camera.*
    C: *The bird **had** already **flown** away.*
       (*The bird had gone before I returned.*)

Also, compare these sentences using **when**:

Simple Past: *When I returned with my camera, the bird **flew** away.* (It went after I returned.)

Past Perfect: *When I returned with my camera, the bird **had flown** away.* (It went before I returned.)

4 The Past Perfect is used in reported speech: *"I have suffered from asthma for many years." She told the doctor that she **had suffered** from asthma for many years.*

(For more on reported speech, see pages 62–65.)

Practice

A Write sentences about what these people had already done or had never done before. Use the Past Perfect, and *already* or *never*.

▶ Last summer Daiyu won a gold medal for the third time.
  She had already won two gold medals before that.

▶ Last year Ken visited Scotland for the first time.
  He had never visited Scotland before that.

1 Last weekend Bryan went curling for the first time.
  He .... before that.

2 Last summer Jeff ran in a marathon for the sixth time.
  He .... before that.

3 Last week Susan wrote a poem for the first time.
  She .... before that.

4 Last week Ann appeared on TV for the first time.
She .... before that.

5 Last summer Tony played tennis at the Rogers Cup for the fifth time.
He .... before that.

6 Last year Jean wrote her third novel.
She .... before that.

B In each case you have two events in the order in which they took place. Write the information in one sentence using the words in parentheses ( ).

▶ A: The driver started the car. B: Ms. Mangeau appeared.
(When Ms. Mangeau/appear/, the driver/already/start/the car)
When Ms. Mangeau appeared, the driver had already started the car. ....

1 A: We put the fire out. B: The firefighters arrived.
(When the firefighters/arrive/, we/already/put/the fire out)
....

2 A: Jim finished the work. B: The manager came back.
(When the manager/come/back, Jim/already/finish/the work)
....

3 A: I went to bed. B: Philip called.
(When Philip/call/, I/already/go/to bed)
....

4 A: Alice and Jack had lunch. B: Their children came home.
(When their children/come/home, Alice and Jack/already/have/lunch)
....

5 A: Ian made dinner. B: His wife got home from work.
(When his wife/get/home from work, Ian/already/make/dinner)
....

6 A: The thieves spent the money. B: The police caught them.
(The thieves/already/spend/the money, when the police/catch/them)
....

C Use the Past Perfect to complete the sentences.

▶ Last summer Pam said, "I've always wanted to fly in a helicopter."
Pam said that she had always wanted to fly in a helicopter. ....

1 Feng said, "Jack has just left."
Feng told us that Jack ....

2 Robert said to Jill, "Have you been to Yellowknife?"
Robert asked Jill if she ....

3 When the boys came home, Mrs. Brock said, "I've made some sandwiches."
Mrs. Brock told the boys that she ....

4 "I know your cousin," said Jacob. "I met her in Charlottetown."
Jacob said he knew my cousin because he ....

5 Bob was talking to Francine, and he said, "Have you ever been to Japan?"
Bob asked Francine if she ....

Will or be going to

Compare **will** and **be going to**:

1 We use **will** with an infinitive (**do, go, be, arrive,** etc.):

> INFINITIVE
> *Marcel* **will arrive** *tomorrow.*

We use **be going** with **to** + infinitive (**to do, to be, to rain,** etc.):

> to + INFINITIVE
> *It's going to snow soon.*
> *My friends are going to come tonight.*
> *It isn't going to snow today.*
> *What are you going to do on Sunday?*

2 We use **will** for actions that we decide to do NOW, at the moment of speaking:

> past   now
> speaking
> decision

> *I like this coat. I think I'll buy it.*
> A: *What would you like to eat?*
> B: *I'll have a pizza, please.*

We can use will for offers and promises:
> *I'll carry your luggage for you.* (OFFER)
> *I won't forget your birthday again.* (PROMISE)

We use **be going to** for actions that we have decided to do BEFORE we speak:

> past   decision   now
> speaking

> *I'm going to clean my room this afternoon.*
> (I decided to clean it this morning.)

We can ask questions about people's plans:
> *Are you going to take the three o'clock train?*
> (= Have you decided to take the three o'clock train?)

3 We use **will** to talk about things that we think or believe will happen in the future:
> *I'm sure you'll enjoy the movie.*
> *I'm sure it won't rain tomorrow. It'll be another beautiful, sunny day.*

We use **be going to** for something that we expect to happen, because the situation now indicates that it is going to happen:
> *He's skating towards the goal, and he's going to score.*

Practice

A Complete the sentences, using the words in parentheses ( ) and *'ll* or a form of *be going to*.

▶ A: Are you going to watch TV tonight?
B: Yes, I'm going to watch......... (I/watch) my favourite show at nine o'clock.

1 A: What .... (you/eat) tonight? What food have you bought?
B: I haven't bought any food.
A: Well, why don't you come to my house? .... (I/cook) us something nice to eat.

2 A: I'm going downtown tomorrow. .... (I/buy) some new clothes.
B: Oh, what .... (you/get)?
A: .... (I/look) for a T-shirt and some jeans.
B: I'd like to go downtown, too. .... (I/come) with you.

3 A: .... (I/leave) work late tomorrow. There is a meeting at six p.m.
B: Oh, I didn't know that. Well, ... (I/see) you after the meeting.

4 .... (I/call) Tom at six o'clock. I promised to call him tonight.

5 A: Are you going to take a vacation in the summer?
B: Yes, ... (I/travel) around Central America with a friend.

B Look at these office scenes. Choose the correct situation for each scene, then choose the correct sentence and cross out the incorrect one.

▶   1   2

3 JAPAN   4 DRINKS   5

a   You look hot, I'll open a window./You look hot, I'm going to open a window.
b   Next year, we're going to enter the Japanese market./Next year, we'll enter the Japanese market.
c   Thanks, I'm going to have an orange juice./Thanks, I'll have an orange juice.
d   Take a break. I'm going to do the photocopying./Take a break. I'll do the photocopying.
e   Relax, I'll answer it./ ~~Relax, I'm going to answer it.~~
f   Thursday is no good for me, I'm afraid. I'll meet the new manager of our Tokyo office./Thursday is no good for me, I'm afraid. I'm going to meet the new manager of our Tokyo office.

C You are at a party. Here are some of the questions you are asked. Reply using *will* or *be going to*.

▶   A: Hi, nice to see you. Would you like a drink?
    B: (I/have/a pop, please) I'll have a pop, please. ....
  1   A: What are you doing these days?
      B: (Nothing much, but I/start/a new job soon) ....
  2   A: Would you like something to eat?
      B: (Thanks, I/have/a sandwich) ....
  3   A: What are your plans for the weekend?
      B: (I/do/some shopping tomorrow and I/go/for a swim on Sunday)
      ....
  4   A: Why is Maria standing by the piano?
      B: (She/sing/, I'm afraid) ....
  5   A: This tourtière looks delicious. Are you going to have some?
      B: (No, but I'm sure you/enjoy/it) ....
  6   A: How are you getting home?
      B: (David/give/me a lift) ....

Future

1 We can talk about future time with different verb forms, for example:

► will: *I'll go with you.*

► be going to: *He's going to go with us.*

► Present Progressive:
We're going tomorrow.

► Simple Present:
When he arrives, we'll have dinner.

2 When we talk about events in the future that we expect to happen but that are not in our control, we can use **will** or **be going to**:
Editha will be (OR *is going to be*) *12 next week.*
We won't see (OR *aren't going to see*) *those birds again until next spring.*
Will they finish (OR *Are they going to finish*) *the building soon?*

3 When we talk about events in the future that are in our control (i.e. we can decide what will happen), we use **will** differently from **be going to**. We use **will** at the time we decide what to do; we use **be going to** after we have decided what to do. Look at these examples:
John: *Can somebody help me, please?*
Helen: *Yes, I'll help you.*
(Here Helen decided <u>after</u> John asked.)

Now compare:
Carol: *John needs some help.*
Helen: *I know. I'm going to help him.*
(Here Helen had decided <u>before</u> Carol spoke.)

4 Look at these examples:
If it rains, they'll stay (OR *they're going to stay*) *at home.*
We'll have (OR *we're going to have*) *lunch after the show ends.*

When a sentence has two parts that refer to the future, we use the Simple Present after **if**, **when**, **before**, **after**, **as soon as**, and **until**, and in the other part of the sentence we use **will** or **be going to**:

When/ after etc.	+	SIMPLE PRESENT	+	will/ be going to
After		*it finishes*		*we'll have lunch.*

5 We use the Present Progressive to talk about a future arrangement that we have made with someone else:
A: *Can you come and see us this evening?*
B: *I can't. I'm playing squash with Sam.*

Cheoul Su can't go to the theatre with us tonight because he's meeting Maria for dinner.

Practice

A Liz has come back to Saskatoon from Mexico. Her brother Tom has just met her at the airport. In the sentences below, think about when the person decides to do something. Put a check if you think the phrase <u>underlined</u> is correct. Otherwise, write the correct form of *will* or *be going to*.

Tom: Hi Liz. Do you want some coffee or water after your trip?

Liz: Thanks. <u>I'll</u> (►)✓............. have a coffee.

Tom: <u>I'm going to</u> (►) <u>I'll</u>............. carry your bag – you look tired. <u>We'll</u> (1)............... go to that coffee shop, over there. Here we are. So, welcome back to Canada. How was Mexico?

Liz: Well, it was great to have some time to think, and I've made some decisions. <u>I'll</u> (2)............... talk to the boss tomorrow, and I'll (3)............... ask him if I can move to another department.

Tom: Good. I'm sure <u>he'll</u> (4)............... give you what you want. Now, would you like something to eat?

Liz: Um, yes. <u>I'm going to</u> (5)............... have a doughnut. Thanks. What about you?

Tom: No, thanks, I don't want to spoil my appetite. I've reserved a table for this evening at the Indian restaurant on Main Street. <u>I'll</u> (6)............... take Giuliana. What are you going to do this evening?

Liz: I haven't thought about it. <u>I'll</u> (7)............... probably cook something. Oh, and I must call Dad. Did you remember that it's his birthday tomorrow?

Tom: Yes, I remembered. <u>He'll</u> (8)............... be fifty. Promise me you'll relax a bit?

Liz: Sure.

Tom: OK. <u>I'll</u> (9)............... get you a taxi. Call me tomorrow. <u>You won't</u> (10)............... forget, will you?

B **Use the words in parentheses ( ) to write sentences using *will* and the Simple Present.**

▶ (Victor/help/us/when/he/come/home) *Victor will help us when he comes home.*...........

1 (I/buy/the tickets/before/I/go/to work) ....

2 (As soon as/Jacques/arrive/, we/have/something to eat) ....

3 (The play/start/after/the music/stop) ....

4 (He/not/stop/until/he/finish/the job) ....

5 (When John/get/here, we/go/to the beach) ....

C **Look at Ann's agenda for next week.**

	MORNING	AFTERNOON/EVENING
Monday	10:00 take Stefano to the airport	wash the car
Tuesday	buy some stamps	mail some packages
Wednesday	11:00 take the dog to the vet	clean my apartment
Thursday	12:30 cook lunch for Mom	buy new snowshoes
Friday	9:00 go snowshoeing with Mary	do the grocery shopping
Saturday	wash my hair	6:00 meet Stefano at the airport

If Ann has plans with someone else, use the Present Progressive, but if she does not, use *be going to*.

▶ Ann <u>is taking</u>..................... Stefano to the airport on Monday morning

▶ On Monday evening Ann <u>is going to wash</u>............. the car.

1 On Tuesday she .... some stamps because she ....
   some packages.

2 She can't see anyone on Wednesday morning because she .... the
   dog to the vet.

3 On Wednesday evening she .... her apartment.

4 On Thursday afternoon she .... new snowshoes because
   .... snowshoeing with Mary on Friday morning.

5 On Friday afternoon she .... the grocery shopping

6 She .... her hair on Saturday morning because she
   .... Stefano at the airport at six o'clock.

Second Conditional (Unreal Conditional)

1 Look at this sentence:

> *If Mary Pickford **were** alive today, she **would be** over 100 years old.*

Of course, Pickford isn't alive today. The sentence imagines something that is not true. The verb after **if** is generally in the Simple Past*, but it refers to the present. This structure is called the Second Conditional:

If + SIMPLE PAST	+ **would** (or **'d**)
If	*he **worked** harder,*	*he **would do** better.*

*See number 4 for an exception.

Another example is someone who doesn't have enough money to buy a new car and says:

*I'**d buy** a new car if I **had** enough money.*

Note that we do not use a comma (,) before **if**.

2 We can use the same type of sentence to talk about the future:

If + SIMPLE PAST	+ **would** (or **'d**)
If	*I **won** a lot of money,*	*I'**d buy** a big house.*

This sentence describes an unlikely future situation: it is unlikely that I will win a lot of money.

3 We can use **wish** to say that we want something to be different from how it is now. Note that the verb after **wish** is in the Simple Past (e.g. **could, was, had**):

I wish you could talk

*I **wish** (that) Pickford **was** still alive.
Claudia **wishes** she **had** enough money for a new dress.
I **wish** I **was** very rich.*

4 After **if** and after **wish**, we sometimes use I/he/she/it with **were**:

> *If he **were** alive today, …
> I wish Mary Pickford **were** still alive.*

Notice also the expression **if I were you**, when you give someone advice:

> *If I **were** you, I'**d** go to the police.*
> (NOT ~~If I was you,~~ …)

Practice

A **Complete these sentences.**

▶ If Paulette lived in Montreal, she _would be_............. (she/be) near her parents.

▶ Fred would read more if _he didn't work_....... (he/not/work) so hard.

1 If Elizabeth didn't have to work in the evenings, ... (she/go) to concerts.

2 Vera wouldn't go to work by car if .... (she/live) near a subway station.

3 Dave wouldn't be overweight if .... (he/not/eat) so much.

4 If Peter didn't live in an apartment, ... (he/have) a dog.

5 Pam would definitely learn Italian if .... (she/get) a job in Italy.

6 If Mark wanted to be healthy, ... (he/not/smoke).

B In the next few years:

> It is unlikely that astronauts will visit Mars.
> It is unlikely that governments will stop buying weapons.
> It is unlikely that scientists will reverse global warming.
> It is unlikely that they will discover oil in Ireland.
> It is unlikely that teenagers will stop downloading movies.

Now use the predictions in the box to complete these sentences.

▶ If <u>governments stopped buying weapons</u> .... , the world would be safer.

1 If .... , the Irish would be very happy.

2 If .... , this terrible problem would disappear.

3 If .... , they might go to the theatre more often.

4 If .... , we would learn a lot about the planet.

C A manager tells people why they can't have a job. Write their thoughts with *I wish*.

▶ You don't have a driver's licence, so you can't have the job.
I wish <u>I had a driver's licence.</u> ....

▶ You can't have the job because you can't type quickly.
I wish <u>I could type quickly.</u> ....

1 You can't have the job because you don't have good eyesight.
I wish ....

2 You can't speak Mandarin, so you can't have the job.
I wish ....

3 You don't have a degree, so you can't have the job.
I wish ....

4 You can't have the job because you are not eighteen.
I wish ....

D Imagine how life nowadays could be better. Complete the sentences using the words in parentheses ( ), and any other words you need.

▶ People don't get enough exercise, so there is a lot of heart disease.
(more, less) If people <u>got more exercise</u> .... , there <u>would be less</u> ....
heart disease.

1 There are too many cars. The city is very polluted.
(fewer) I wish there .... , then the city wouldn't be very polluted.

2 People drive too fast, so there are a lot of accidents.
(more slowly) I wish people .... , then there would be fewer
accidents.

3 People watch too much TV, so they don't have much time for reading.
(more) If people watched less TV, they ....

4 Children have cavities because they eat too much candy.
(less) Children would have fewer cavities if they ....

5 Not enough people travel by public transit, so the roads are crowded.
(more) I wish .... , then the roads would be less crowded.

6 People don't have enough time to cook, so they eat a lot of fast food.
(more, less) If people .... , they ....

Third Conditional (Past Conditional)

1 Look at this sentence:

> If Mary Pickford **had died** in 1992, she **would have been** 100 years old.

Pickford did not in fact die in 1992. She died before she was 100 years old. The sentence imagines something that did not happen in the past. This structure is called the Third Conditional:

> If + PAST PERFECT + would have (or 'd have) + past participle
> If he **had tried** harder, he **would have won**.

Here is another example:

> If Keisha **had come** on her usual bus, I **would have seen** her. (She didn't come on her usual bus, so I didn't see her.)

Notice how we can also use the negative forms **wouldn't have** and **hadn't**:

> John F. Kennedy **wouldn't have died** in 1963 if he **hadn't gone** to Dallas. (Kennedy died in 1963 because he went to Dallas, but this sentence imagines the opposite.)
> I **would have called** you if I **hadn't lost** your phone number. (I didn't call you because I lost your phone number.)
> I **wouldn't have gone** to the museum if I had known it was closed. (I went to the museum because I didn't know it was closed.)

2 We can use **wish + had done** to talk about the past when we are sorry that something didn't happen, and we imagine that it did:

> He **wishes** he **had studied** harder at school. (He didn't study hard, and now he's sorry about it.)
> I woke up very late this morning. I **wish** I **had gone** to bed earlier last night.

We can use a negative form (**wish ... hadn't done**) to say that we are sorry that something did happen:

> Many people **wish** that John F. Kennedy **hadn't gone** to Dallas. (Many people are sorry that John F. Kennedy went to Dallas.)

Practice

A Read this story about Anita.

In May 2008 Anita lost her job in Edmonton. She didn't have much money in the bank, so she was very worried. She looked in the newspapers and she saw an advertisement for a job as a translator from French into English. She didn't speak French very well, so she didn't apply for it. In June, she heard about some teaching jobs overseas because a friend called to tell her about them. She called the company, and they asked her to go for an interview with the director. Anita thought the interview went badly, but in fact the director was happy with the interview and offered Anita a job in Japan. However, Anita couldn't start immediately because she didn't know any Japanese. She took a course to learn the language. She was good at languages and she made rapid progress. So, by September she had a new job, and she still had a little money left in the bank.

Now write sentences using the words in parentheses ( ).

▶ (If Anita/have/a lot of money in the bank, she/not/be/so worried.)

  If Anita had had a lot of money in the bank, she wouldn't have been so worried.

▶ (If she/not/look/in the newspapers, she/not/see/the advertisement.)

  If she hadn't looked in the newspapers, she wouldn't have seen the advertisement.

1 (If she/speak/French very well, she/apply/for the job.)

....

2 (If her friend/not/call, she/not/hear/about the teaching jobs.)

....

3 (If she/not/contact/the company, they/not/ask/her to go for an interview.)

....

4 (If the interview/go/badly, the director/not/offer/Anita a job.)

....

5 (If Anita/know/some Japanese, she/start/immediately.)

....

6 (If she/not/be/good at languages, she/not/make/rapid progress.)

....

B Use the information in parentheses ( ) to complete these sentences.

▶ (Sam didn't get the job as a translator because he failed the test.)
Sam _would have gotten_. the job as a translator if he _had_.................. not
failed.................. the test.

1 (Maurice lost our phone number, so he didn't call us.)
If Maurice .... not .... phone number, he
.... us.

2 (Bella broke her leg, so she didn't go on vacation.)
If Bella .... not .... her leg, she ....
on vacation.

3 (We didn't make a cake because we forgot to buy some eggs.)
We .... a cake if we .... not ....
to buy some eggs.

C Write sentences about these people who are sorry about things they did in the past.
Use *wish* or *wishes*.

▶ Josh wasted his time at school; now he's sorry.
Josh wishes he hadn't wasted his time at school...

1 I didn't tell the truth; now I'm sorry.
I wish ....

2 John borrowed some money from his mother; now he's sorry.
John ....

3 Jenny didn't get up early; now she's sorry.
Jenny ....

4 Dino didn't go to the party; now he's sorry.
Dino ....

5 I didn't send Betty a birthday card; now I'm sorry.
I ....

6 Fiona didn't help her sister; now she's sorry.
....

7 He shouted at the children; now he's sorry.
....

Make, do, have, get

1   There are many phrases in which a particular verb is used together with a particular noun, for example:
    make a cup of coffee
    do some work
    have breakfast

2   We often use **make** in sentences about producing or creating something:
    *They **made** a fire in the woods.*
    *Shall I **make** some coffee?*
    *He **made** some sandwiches for lunch.*

3   We also use **make** in these phrases:
    *Excuse me. I have to **make** a phone call.*
    *He **makes** a lot of mistakes in his work.*
    *I couldn't sleep because the neighbours were **making** a lot of noise.*
    *You should **make** your bed in the morning.*

4   We often use **do** in sentences about working, or about particular jobs:
    *Have you **done** your homework?*
    *He offered to **do** the dishes.*
    *We're going to **do** some shopping.*
    *I haven't **done** much work today.*

5   We use **have** + **noun** to describe activities:
    *We usually **have** lunch at about one o'clock.*
    *I'm **having** fish for dinner tonight.*
    *I **had** a nap in the park this afternoon.*

6   We use **get** with adjectives that describe feelings, to say that we begin to have the feeling:
    *I'm **getting** tired now. I need a break.*
    *They're late and I'm **getting** worried.*
    *I **got** angry and shouted at them.*

7   We use **get** in some phrases that describe a change of situation:
    *We **got** lost in Toronto. (= We became lost …)*
    *It's **getting** cold. (= It's becoming cold.)*
    *Jane was very sick, but she's **getting** better.*
    *They **got** married three years ago.*
    *It rained heavily and I **got** very wet.*

8   We use **make** + **someone** + **adjective** to talk about the cause of a feeling:
    *He **made** us very angry.*
    *The news **made** him happy.*

Practice

A   Complete the sentences, using the correct forms of *make*, *do*, *have*, or *get*. Be careful that you use the correct tense.

▶   He was *making*........ a cup of coffee in the kitchen.

▶   We *had*........... lunch in a very nice little restaurant yesterday.

1   She always .... excited before her birthday.

2   A: Helen's sick.
    B: Oh no. I hope she will .... better soon.

3   We have to .... some homework every day.

4   I think I've .... a terrible mistake.

5   They .... the grocery shopping and then they went home.

6   I was late because I .... lost on my way there.

7   It always .... very hot here during the summer.

8   Could I .... a quick phone call, please?

9   Please don't .... so much noise.

10 It was a lovely surprise and it .... me very happy.

11 Her parents are .... old. They are sixty or seventy.

12 How old were you when you .... married?

B Look at the notes in the box about what Laura did yesterday. Complete the sentences, using the correct forms of *make, do, have,* or *get*. Sometimes more than one answer is possible.

7:30	Got up. Bed.
8:00	Breakfast (orange juice and toast).
8:30–9:00	Walk to work. Rain.
9:00–1:00	Work. Very busy.
1:00–2:00	Lunch in office. Sandwiches.
2:00–5:00	Work. Finished everything.
5:30	Shopping. Home.
7:00	Pizza for dinner. Dishes.
8:00–11:00	TV. Tired. Bed.

It was a normal day for Laura yesterday. She got up at 7:30 and she (►) made......... the bed. Then she (1)............... breakfast. For breakfast she (2)............... orange juice and toast. While she was walking to work, it rained and she (3)............... wet. She (4)............... angry about this. In the morning she (5)............... a lot of work. She (6)............... lunch at about one o'clock. She (7)............... sandwiches for lunch. When she had (8)............... all her work in the afternoon, she went home. On the way home she (9)............... some shopping. She (10)............... a pizza for dinner. She (11)............... the dishes and then she watched TV for three hours. By eleven o'clock she felt tired, and so she went to bed.

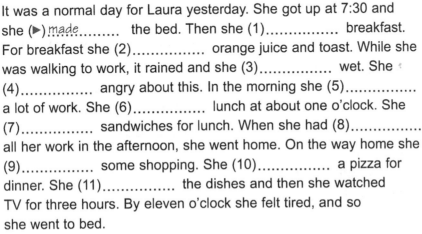

C Complete the dialogues, using the correct form of *make, do, have,* or *get*.

► A: Was the movie good?
   B: No, I got........... bored in the middle of it.

1 A: Could you .... some shopping for me?
   B: Yes, what do you want me to buy?

2 A: Were you pleased by the news?
   B: No, it .... me very unhappy.

3 A: Was it a warm day?
   B: Yes, but it .... very cold in the evening.

4 A: Are you hungry right now?
   B: No, I .... a big meal a couple of hours ago.

5 A: Did he pass the test?
   B: No, he .... a lot of mistakes.

6 A: Are you ready to go out?
   B: No, I'm not. I want to .... a load of laundry first.

7 A: Could you fix this for me?
   B: Yes, but I can't .... the job until tomorrow.

Phrasal verbs (1): meanings and types

1 We can use many verbs together with another word to form phrasal verbs, e.g. **put on, get up.**

The same verb can go with several different words to form phrasal verbs with different meanings, e.g. **put away, put on, put through.**

The meaning of a phrasal verb is not always clear from the two parts. For example, **put through** means connect (= to make a telephone connection). You should check the meaning of phrasal verbs in a dictionary.

2 Grammatically, there are three types of phrasal verbs.

▸ One type consists of **verb + adverb** and they have an object, e.g.:
  She put on the hat.
  She put the hat on.

Some common verbs of this type are:

> **bring up, calm down, cross out, fill in, find out, give in, give out, look up, pick up, point out, pull off, put away, put through, take off, try on, turn off, work out**

▸ The second type of phrasal verb consists of **verb + adverb** but there is no object, e.g.
  I usually get up at seven o'clock.

Some common verbs of this type are:

> **break down, check in, get off, get up, go on, go out, hand in, hang around, look out, set off, show up, stay up, take off, turn out, turn up**

▸ The third type consists of **verb + adverb + preposition** and they have an object, e.g.:
  We're looking forward to your news.

Some common verbs of this type are:

> **do away with, face up to, run out of, look up to**

(See also pages 34–35.)

Practice

A Complete these dialogues with the phrasal verb and a pronoun.

▸ A: Has Amanda put her hat on? B: Yes, she's <u>put it on</u> .
1 A: Who brought up the children? B: Their uncle ....
2 A: Did you cross out the wrong words? B: No, the teacher ....
3 A: When do we have to hand in the homework? B: We have to .... tomorrow.
4 A: Can you pick Wayne up after school? B: OK, I'll .... on my way home.
5 A: Children, put your toys away now, please. B: Can't we .... later?

B Rewrite each sentence, replacing the <u>underlined expression</u> with the correct form of one of the phrasal verbs from the box.

> break down, give out, go on, keep off, ~~look out~~, look up to, put through

▸ <u>Be careful</u>! Don't step into the hole!
  <u>Look out</u> .... ! Don't step into the hole!

1 The young boys really <u>admire</u> the hockey players.

   The young boys really .... the hockey players.

2 The teacher <u>distributed</u> the test papers.

   The teacher .... the test papers.

3 Wait one moment. I'll try to <u>connect</u> you.

   Wait one moment. I'll try to .... you ....

4 What's <u>happening</u> here? What are you doing?

   What's .... here? What are you doing?

5 Jim's old car <u>stopped working</u> completely last weekend.

   Jim's old car .... completely last weekend.

6 Mr. Gaston yelled at the boys, "<u>Don't walk on</u> my lawn."

   Mr. Gaston yelled at the boys, "........................ my lawn."

C **Sally and Gelina are staying in Toronto and are planning to do some shopping. Complete the dialogue with the correct form of the phrasal verbs in the box. Use a dictionary to check the meanings.**

> find out (x2), get off, look up, put on, run out of, head out, take off, try on

Sally: Have you (▶)_found out_........... where the best shopping area is?

Gelina: Yes, I (1)........................ it .... in the guidebook. We can get on
         the subway right across the street and we (2)........................ at Queen Street.

Sally: By the way, I've (3)........................ cash so we'll have to stop at a bank.

Gelina: We can go to the hotel reception and (4)........................ if there's an ATM near
         here. What are you going to wear?

Sally: If we're going to (5)........................ clothes, I think I'll wear a skirt. It's more
         difficult to (6)........................ jeans and (7)........................ them
         .... all the time.

Gelina: OK, as soon as you've changed we can (8)........................ .

D **Complete the following story by choosing the second word of each phrasal verb. Use a dictionary to check the meanings**

We were looking forward (▶) to/~~on~~ our vacation but the night before we were going to
leave we stayed (1) down/up talking until about three o'clock. We didn't hear the alarm
clock so we got (2) up/in late and we were late getting to the airport. When we went to
check (3) in/up, we were lucky because some passengers hadn't shown (4) up/out so
there were still some seats left. When we got on the plane, Tim was a bit nervous
because he hadn't flown before but I gave him a pill and that calmed him (5) down/out.
The cabin crew told us to turn (6) in/off our cellphones. Then the lights went (7) up/off
and Tim thought something was wrong but I pointed (8) out/up that they always do that
before the plane takes (9) out/off. When we got to Mexico City we went to pick (10)
up/off our bags. Mine was one of the first to come out, but Tim's didn't appear. We hung
(11) around/up for a long time but it didn't turn (12) out/up. We went to an office to report
it and Tim had to fill (13) in/on all his details on a form. After several phone calls it turned
(14) out/up that Tim's bag was in Atlanta. Luckily, we got it back that same evening.
As soon as it arrived, Tim pulled (15) out/off his sweaty clothes, had a cold shower
and put (16) in/on a clean shirt and pants. We were just in time to go and have dinner.

Phrasal verbs (2): separability

1 Grammatically, phrasal verbs fall into three groups. Some phrasal verbs can belong to different groups, (see pages 32–33) sometimes with different meanings. For example, **clear up**:

*Who's going to **clear up** this misunderstanding?*
(= remove confusion)
*The weather soon **cleared up**.*
(= improved)

2 Verbs in the first group consist of **verb + adverb** and they have an object. When the object is a noun, there are two possible positions, e.g.:

*Frank **cleared up** the misunderstanding.*
*Frank **cleared** the misunderstanding **up**.*

However, when the object is a pronoun, it goes between the two parts of the verb, e.g.
*Frank **cleared** it **up**.* (NOT: Frank cleared up it.)

Some common verbs in this group are:

> break off, carry on, cut out, draw out, get off, give up, lay off, let out, make up, put on, set up, shut down, sort out, tear down, turn on

3 Verbs in the second group consist of **verb + adverb** but there is no object, e.g.:
*Where did you **grow up**?*

Some common verbs in this group are:

> call in, come about, cut down, go on, hang on, look out, stay in, stop by

4 Verbs in the third group consist of **verb + adverb + preposition** and they have an object, e.g.:
*I can't **put up with** all this noise.*

Some common verbs in this group are:

> do away with, face up to, get away with, put up with

Practice

A Complete these dialogues with the phrasal verb and a pronoun.

► A: Has somebody turned the lights on?
  B: I think Joe *turned them on* .

1 A: When did they tear down the theatre?
  B: They .... several months ago.

2 A: Look at this skirt! How can I get the ink off?
  B: I think the only way to .... is to take it to the cleaner's.

3 A: I need to find someone to let out my new dress.
  B: I know an excellent seamstress who can ....

4 A: Sarita and Pete have broken off their engagement.
  B: Oh! When did they .... ?

B Replace the <u>underlined expression</u> in each sentence with the correct form of one of the phrasal verbs from the box.

> get away with, hang on, put up with, sort out, stop by, ~~tear down~~

► They're going to <u>demolish</u> those old houses.
  They're going to *tear down* .... those old houses.

1 The gang <u>escaped taking</u> 5 million dollars.
   The gang .... 5 million dollars.
2 I'm going out. I can't <u>stand</u> the noise in here.
   I'm going out. I can't .... the noise in here.
3 Marjorie says she's going to <u>visit us</u> on Thursday.
   Marjorie says she's going to .... on Thursday.
4 <u>Wait!</u> I've just got to get my jacket.
   .... ! I've just got to get my jacket.
5 We still haven't <u>arranged</u> who will do the different jobs.
   We still haven't .... who will do the different jobs.

C Complete this interview by writing the correct form of one of the phrasal verbs in each blank.

> come about, cut down, do away with, face up to, give up, go on, ~~grow up~~, lay off, let out, make up, put in, set up, shut down, stay in, stop by, take out, take over

Interviewer: I understand that your early life was not easy. Can you tell us a little about it? Where were you born?
Ruth: In Hearst, in northern Ontario; and that's where I (►) _grew up_ .
Interviewer: Were you lonely as a child?
Ruth: I had three sisters and two brothers so it was never quiet. There was always something (1)........................ . The house was never empty because neighbours (2)........................ all the time.
Interviewer: Do you remember any particularly happy moments?
Ruth: Yes, when we went to bed my mother always told us stories. She didn't have a book – she just (3)........................ them .... herself.
Interviewer: And then things went wrong. How did that (4)........................ ?
Ruth: Well, to start with, my father smoked a lot. He always said that he was going to (5)........................ , but he never did. He got very sick and he was in the hospital for several weeks. Even when the doctor (6)........................ him .... , he wasn't well. He had to (7)........................ and keep warm so that his bronchitis wouldn't start again. But at least he had the sense to finally (8)........................ smoking.
Interviewer: But things got worse.
Ruth: Yes, while he was recovering we heard that the factory where he worked had (9)........................ a lot of workers. At first he wasn't affected but then we heard that they were going to (10)........................ the factory ....
Interviewer: And then things got better.
Ruth: Yes, my parents had to (11)........................ their new situation. They said that businesses could (12)........................ factory workers but they would always need office staff. Luckily they had a savings account and every week they had (13)........................ something .... Now they decided to (14)........................ their savings and (15)........................ a little business selling office equipment. It did quite well and when they retired I decided to (16)........................ it ....
Interviewer: Well, that is a story with a happy ending. Thank you for speaking to me.

Must, can't, may, might, could

1   We use **must**, **can't**, **may** and **could** with an infinitive (e.g. be, go, come, earn):

$$\text{They } must \boxed{\begin{array}{c}\text{INFINITIVE}\\ earn\end{array}} a\ lot.$$

2 CERTAINTY $\boxed{\textit{She \textbf{must be} rich.}}$

Look at this example with **must**: *Maureen got high marks in her classes. She **must be** very smart.* (= From what we know, we can be certain that Maureen is very smart.)

We use **must** to say we are certain:
> *The Greens have two houses and two cars. They **must earn** a lot of money.*
> (= We can be sure that the Greens earn a lot of money.)
> A: *There's someone outside in an orange car.*
> B: *It **must be** Geraldine. She's the only person I know with an orange car.*

3 IMPOSSIBILITY $\boxed{\textit{She \textbf{can't be} poor.}}$

Look at this example with **can't**:
> *Mark studied hard for his tests, but he got a low grade; he **can't be** very smart.*
> (= From what we know, we can guess that Mark is **not** very smart.)

We use **can't** to talk about impossibility:
> *The Browns both have part-time jobs; they **can't earn** much money.* (= We can guess that the Browns do **not** earn a lot of money.)
> A: *There's someone at the door. I think it's Bill.*
> B: *It **can't be** Bill. He's in Nanaimo.*

4 POSSIBILITY

$$\text{She } \left\{\begin{array}{c} may\\ might\\ could\end{array}\right\} be\ in\ the\ yard.$$

Look at this example with **may**:
> A: *Eve's not in her room. Where is she?*
> B: *She **may be** in the yard.* (= From what we know, **perhaps** she **is** in the yard.)

We use **may**, **might** and **could** for something that is possible but not certain, now or in the future:
> *My sister **might come** tomorrow.* (= From what we know, perhaps she **will** come.)

Now look at this example with **may not**:
> A: *I called Teresa, but there was no answer.*
> B: *She **may not be** at home.* (OR *She **might not be** …*) (= Perhaps she is not at home.)

Could not is not possible here.

Practice

A Complete the sentences using *must* or *can't* and one of the verbs from the box.

~~be~~	belong	~~speak~~	come	spend	have	like	live	want	remember

▶ Anna lived in Rome for three years, so she <u>must speak</u> Italian.
▶ Kumar's brother doesn't know anything about medicine, so he <u>can't be</u>...... a doctor.
1 Jane has an incredible number of DVDs. She .... movies a lot.
2 Peter doesn't speak German, so he .... from Germany.
3 This jacket .... to Colleen because it's not her size.
4 That man .... around here because he doesn't know any of the street names.
5 Jack .... a lot of clothes. He wears something different every day.
6 Sam's grandmother is over 80 years old, so she .... the Second World War.
7 You've got ten cats already. You .... to get another one.
8 Sasha buys a new dress every day. She .... a lot of money on clothes.

B Someone has robbed a bank. The police are sure that the criminal is one of these men. Look at the pictures and complete the sentences using *can't be*, *could be*, or *must be*.

Drake Hall Brown Rogers Smith

▶ A witness says that the robber had short hair. If that's true, then it *can't be* Drake or Rogers, but it *could be* Hall.

▶ A witness says that the robber had glasses. If that's true, then it *can't be* Brown or Drake. It *must be* either Hall or Rogers or Smith.

1 A witness says that the robber had black hair. If that's true, then it .... Hall, but it .... Brown.

2 A witness says that the robber had a moustache. If that's true, then it .... Rogers but it .... Drake or Brown.

3 A witness says that the robber didn't have a beard. If that's true, then it .... Drake or Brown but it .... Hall or Smith.

4 A witness says that the robber had a moustache, but no beard. If that's true, then it .... Drake or Rogers. It .... Hall.

5 A witness says that the robber had black hair and wore glasses. If that's true, then it .... Rogers. It .... Hall.

6 And if what everyone says is true, then it ....

C Complete the dialogues with *must*, *can't*, or *might* and one of the phrases in the box.

cost a lot of money	~~be a soldier~~	work long hours	go to Portugal
come this weekend	take much interest	also be at the mall	be at the gym

▶ Ruth: I think Ann's brother is in the army.
Brian: He *can't be a soldier* ; he's only 15.

1 Bob: What are you going to do next summer?
Susan: I don't know. We .... , but it's not certain yet.

2 Sanjit: Mike's new apartment is all electric – kitchen, heating, everything.
Peter: That .... in electricity bills.

3 Sam: Is Mary coming to see us this week?
Sally: It depends on her work. She .... if she finishes the project that she's doing.

4 Carol: Have Brian and Kim got any children?
John: Yes, they have two children, but they .... in them, because they never talk about them.

5 Andrew: Do you see your new neighbours very much?
Sarah: No, they .... , because they are hardly ever at home.

6 Greg: Fred went out, didn't he? Where has he gone?
Ann: I don't know. He .... or he ....

Must/have to, must not/don't have to

1 We use **must** when the speaker thinks it is necessary or important to do an action:
> *You must go.* (= It is important that you go.)

We make negatives, questions, and short answers like this:
> *You must not go.*
> *Must you go? ~ Yes, I must.*

2 We use **have to** to talk about an action that is necessary because of rules or laws, or because someone obliges us to do it:
> *Doctors sometimes have to work on Sunday.*

We make negatives, questions, and short answers with a form of **do**:
> *Teachers don't have to work on Sunday.*
> *Do you have to work today? ~ No, I don't.*

3 POSITIVE
In positive sentences we can often use **must** and **have to** with little difference in meaning, because many things are important both because we think so and because there are rules:
> *You must work hard in order to succeed*
> (OR ... *you have to work* ...).

4 NEGATIVE
Note the difference in meaning between **must not** and **don't have to**.

In negative sentences we often use **must not** to say that something is against the rules, or against the law:
> *You must not smoke on buses.* (Smoking is against the rules.)
> *In soccer you must not touch the ball with your hands.* (Touching the ball is against the rules.)

We use **don't have to** to say that people are not obliged to do something:
> *In Canada, people don't have to carry a passport with them.* (= People are not obliged to carry one.)
> *Nowadays students do not have to learn Latin at school.* (= They are not obliged to learn it.)

5 QUESTIONS
In questions we usually use **do/does ... have to** (NOT ~~must~~) to ask if something is obligatory or important:
> *Does Michael have to get up early tomorrow?*
> *Do we have to wait here?*

Practice

A The Stanton Squash Club has decided that it is important for all club members to do these things:

> wear sports shoes and clean clothes   have a shower   pay before you play   finish on time

But these things are not allowed:

> disturb other players   eat or drink outside the restaurant   take club balls home

Write *have to*, *don't have to*, or *must not* in the blanks.

▶ You *don't have to* .... wear white clothes, but you *have to* .... wear sports shoes.

▶ You *must not* .... disturb other players, but you *don't have to* .... be silent.

1 You .... finish on time, but you .... start on time.

2 You .... play with club balls, but if you do, you .... take them home.

3 You .... eat or drink outside the restaurant, but you .... buy your food in the restaurant if you don't want to.

4 You .... have a shower, and you .... wear clean clothes.

B Read the signs and complete the sentences with *don't have to* or *must not*.

ANTIQUES
Please feel free to come in.
(No eating inside.)

▶ You *don't have to* go in.
▶ You *must not* eat inside.

Entry possible
30 minutes
before the concert.
No late arrivals
allowed.

1 .... arrive half an hour early.
2 You .... arrive late.

All vehicles – **slow**.
Drivers of large
vehicles, wait for
guard before crossing.

3 Small vehicles .... wait.
4 Drivers of large vehicles .... cross alone.

STUDENTS!
**Please be quiet –
4th-year exam
in progress.**

5 Students .... make any noise.
6 Third-year students .... take the exam.

LIBRARY
No talking.
Please leave books
on tables.

7 You .... talk in the library.
8 You .... put the books back on the shelves.

SWIMMING POOL
Free swim today.
No eating.
No drinking.

9 Swimmers .... pay today.
10 Swimmers .... eat or drink by the pool.

C Write the words from the box in the blanks. Don't add any other words.

Does she	have to	has	she has	must	must not	~~have~~	does she

Mark: We (▶) *have* to get up early tomorrow.
Bob: Why?
Mark: Have you forgotten? Angela (1)................ to move to a new apartment tomorrow,
and I promised we would help her.
Bob: (2)................ have to move out by a particular time?
Mark: No, there's no rush. She doesn't (3)................ leave her old apartment before the
afternoon, but there are lots of things that (4)................ to pack, so we
(5)................ get there fairly early.
Bob: Why (6)................ have to move, by the way?
Mark: She said that I (7)................ tell you because she wants to tell you herself, when
she sees you tomorrow.

Need, doesn't need, didn't need to

1 We use the verb **need** to talk about things that we must do. We use to + infinitive (e.g. **to do, to go**) after **need**:

| I **need** | **to + INFINITIVE**
to go | to the dentist. |

After **he/she/it** we use **needs**:

*Sonia/she **needs to buy** some white paint.*

We make negatives, questions and short answers with a form of **do**:

*You **don't need to go** to the dentist.*
*Sonia **doesn't need to buy** any green paint.*
A: *Do you **need to go** to the dentist?*
B: *Yes, I **do**./No, I **don't**.*
A: *Does Sonia **need to buy** any brushes?*
B: *Yes, she **does**./No, she **doesn't**.*

2 We can also use **need** to talk about things that we must get. Here we use an object after need:

	OBJECT
*Sonia **needs***	*some white paint.*
*I **need***	*a new car.*
*Does Sri **need***	*any help?*

3 To talk about what we do not need to do, we can use **don't/doesn't need to**. We use an infinitive (e.g. **go, buy**) after **don't/doesn't need to**.

INFINITIVE
*You **don't need to** |go| to the grocery store.*
We have enough food.
*Sonia **doesn't need to buy** any paint.*

4 We can use **needed to** for past time:
*They **needed to clean** everything before they started to paint.*

The negative simple past form is **didn't need to**.
*The room wasn't dirty so they **didn't need to clean it** before they started to paint it.*
   (= It was not necessary to clean the room so they didn't clean it.)

We use **didn't need to** + infinitive to talk about something that **was** done although it wasn't necessary:
*We **didn't need to light** the fire, because it was a warm evening.* (= We lit the fire, but it was not necessary to light it.)
*You **didn't need to buy** any bread, Jim. There is plenty in the kitchen.*
   (= You bought some bread, but it was not necessary.)

Practice

A From the statements in parentheses ( ), create a question and a short answer, like those in the examples.

▶ (Tom needs to take some warm clothes.) <u>Does Tom need to take some warm clothes</u> ? ~ Yes, <u>he does</u> .

▶ (She doesn't need to study hard.) <u>Does she need to study hard</u> ? ~ No, <u>she doesn't</u> .

1 (Fred needs a ladder.) .... ? ~ Yes, ...

2 (We don't need to go to the store.) .... ? ~ No, ...

3 (John doesn't need to leave before lunch.) .... ? ~ No, ...

4 (They need to check the train times.) .... ? ~ Yes, ...

B Change each sentence in parentheses ( ) into a negative sentence with *doesn't/don't need*.

▶ (Jane needs to pay Jim today.) Jane doesn't need to pay Jim today.

▶ (The car needs new tires.) The car doesn't need new tires.

1 (We need a lot of red paper.) ....

2 (Marc-Andre needs to get everything ready today.) ....

3 (Marie needs to leave at six o'clock.) ....

4 (Ann needs a new purse.) ....

C When there are exams or games at Macdonald High School, the school provides certain things for all the students, but there are other things that the school does not provide. Look at the table.

Events	The school provides:	The school doesn't provide:
art exams	paint	brushes
math exams	erasers	pens and pencils
geography exams	paper	rulers and pencils
badminton games	birdies	racquets
hockey games	helmets	skates

Use the information in the table to write sentences with *need to bring* or *don't need to bring*.

▶ (art exams/paint) For art exams, students don't need to bring paint.

▶ (badminton games/racquets) For badminton games, students need to bring racquets.

1 (math exams/pens and pencils) ....

2 (hockey games/helmets) ....

3 (geography exams/paper) ....

4 (art exams/brushes) ....

5 (badminton games/birdies) ....

6 (hockey games/skates) ....

7 (math exams/erasers) ....

8 (geography exams/rulers and pencils) ....

D Rewrite the sentences using *didn't need* + the correct form of the verb.

▶ The courses didn't cost us anything. We didn't pay for them.
   We didn't need to pay for the courses.

▶ You took your umbrella yesterday but it didn't rain.
   You didn't need to take your umbrella yesterday.

1 Daniella paid for her vacation in advance, but it wasn't necessary.
   Daniella .... for her vacation in advance.

2 My sister spoke to Loretta yesterday, so I didn't call her.
   I .... Loretta because my sister had spoken to her.

3 We bought extra food but now Jean and Celeste can't come.
   We .... extra food because Jean and Celeste can't come.

4 Why did you work during the weekend? We don't have to finish until next week.
   You .... during the weekend.

5 I didn't take my passport with me because a driver's licence was enough.
   I .... my passport with me.

Should, ought to, had better

1 We use **should**, **ought to**, and **had better**
with an infinitive (e.g. **be**, **go**, **ask**, **wait**):

	INFINITIVE
I should	*go.*
You ought to	*ask.*
We had better	*wait.*

2 We use both **should** and **ought to** to ask for
or to give advice, to say what is the correct or
best thing to do:

> A: *I've got toothache. What **should** I **do**?*
> (= What is the best thing for me to do?)
> B: *You **should go** to the dentist.*
> (= The best thing for you to do is to go
> to the dentist.)

When we are talking about a duty or a law,
we usually use **ought to**:

> A: *I saw a robbery. What **should** I **do**?*
> B: *You **ought to report** it to the police.*
> (= It is a person's duty to report it.)

On the other hand, when we are giving a
personal opinion, we usually use **should**:

> B: *I think you **should forget** about it.*

We use **should** much more than **ought to** in
negatives and questions:

> *I **shouldn't** go.* (OR *I **ought not to** go.*)
> ***Should** I go?* (OR ***Ought** I **to** go?*)

3 We can also use **had better** to give advice, to
say what is the best thing to do:

> *There'll be a lot of traffic tomorrow. We **had**
> (OR We'**d**) **better leave** early.*
> *I **had** (OR I'**d**) **better ask** the doctor about
> the pain in my stomach.*

Note that **had** is a past form, but it does not
refer to past time here; we use it to talk about
present or future time.

We only use **had better** to give advice about a
particular thing; when we give general
advice, we use **should** or **ought to**:

> *When people are in trouble, they **should go**
> to the police.* (NOT-... ~~they had better go to~~
> ~~the police.~~)

The negative is **had better not**:

> *They **had better not** be late.*

Practice

A Use *should* or *shouldn't* and one of the phrases from the box in each dialogue.

call an ambulance	~~report it to the police~~	move the person yourself
drive home in her car	touch anything	~~do anything about it~~
~~decide for herself~~	give you a new cup	encourage him to play sports
borrow money	leave everything where it is	ask someone to take her
let him eat so much		

▶ A: There is a house near my home where I often hear a child crying.
  B: You *should report it to the police* .

▶ A: My daughter wants to marry an artist. What should I do about it?
  B: In my opinion, *you shouldn't do anything about it* .
    Your daughter *should decide for herself* .

1 A: If someone has a serious accident, what's the right thing to do?
  B: Well, you .... It's not a good idea to move an
    injured person. Instead, you .... to take the person
    to hospital.

2 A: Last Saturday I bought some coffee cups but one of the handles was broken.
   What can I expect the store to do?
   B: They ....
3 A: My son is 12 years old and he's very overweight.
   B: Well, it's important not to eat too much, so you ....
   Also, you ....
4 A: If you come home and see that you've been robbed, what's the best thing to do?
   B: Well, you .... You
   .... and call the police.
5 A: Imelda can't work because she's feeling sick. How can she get home?
   B: Well, she .... She
   .... home.
6 People .... if they can't pay it back.

B Use the sentences in parentheses ( ) to write a reply with *had better* in the following dialogues.

► A: I've got a headache.
   B: (You should go and lie down.) *You'd better go and lie down.*
1 A: The children want to play in the kitchen.
   B: (Well, they should clean everything up when they finish.)
   Well, ... when they finish.
2 A: I think it's going to rain.
   B: (Yes, we ought to take our umbrellas.) Yes, ...
3 A: I'm going to go to bed now. We have to get up very early tomorrow.
   B: (Yes, I should go to bed early, too.) Yes, ...

C Complete the second part of the dialogue using the correct form of the word in parentheses ( ). Write *to* or *not* in the correct place if necessary.

► A: Should Henry stay in bed?
   B: No, the doctor said he *shouldn't* .... (should) stay in bed.
1 A: Can we move that cabinet?
   B: No, it's very delicate, so you .... (ought) leave it where it is.
2 A: Should we change these signs?
   B: No, the show is still on, so we .... (should) change them until next week.
3 A: You'd better tell the boss about the accident immediately.
   B: No, she's in a bad mod. I .... (had better) tell her until tomorrow.
4 A: Does the doctor say it's all right for Mrs. Liu to work?
   B: Yes, but she must be careful. She .... (ought) lift anything heavy, for example.
5 A: Can they come before dinner?
   B: No, we haven't got enough food, so they .... (had better) come after dinner.

Had to ..., should have ...

1 Look at this example:

*Jane **had to wait** an hour for a bus.*

Had to wait means that Jane waited because no bus came for an hour.

We use **had to** to talk about something that someone did because it was necessary.

If someone did not do something because it was not necessary, we use **didn't have to**:
*I **didn't have to work** last Saturday. (= I didn't work because it was not necessary.)*

The question form is **did ... have to**:
*Did you **have to work** last Saturday?*

2 Now consider this situation:

> Preema's job includes working on Saturday. Last Saturday she was sick, so she didn't work:
> *Preema **should have gone** to work last Saturday, but she was sick. So she stayed at home.*

We use **should have** (**done/gone**, etc.) to say that something which did not happen was the correct or best action. We can also use **should have** to criticize someone. Look at this example:

> Peter, a farm worker, didn't close a gate, and the cows got into the wrong field:
> *Peter **should have closed** the gate.*

We use **shouldn't have** (**done/gone**, etc.) to say that something which did happen was not the correct action:
*I **shouldn't have gotten** angry with Alvaro. (= I got angry with Alvaro, but it was not a good thing to do.)*
*Peter **shouldn't have left** the gate open.*

Practice

A Complete the dialogues with *had to* or *did ... have to* and the words in parentheses ( ).

▶ Brodie: When you had that stomach trouble, <u>did you have to</u> .... (you) go to the hospital?

Joan: No, I <u>didn't have to</u> .... (not) go to the hospital, but I <u>had to</u> .... stay in bed for a week.

1 Alan: Was there a translation question on the exam?

Jane: No, we .... (not) translate anything, but we .... write three essays.

2 Carrie: I was very busy yesterday.

Jeff: What .... (you) do?

Carrie: I .... prepare everything for today's meeting.

3 Ken: .... (you) wear a uniform when you were in school?

Jean: Yes, and we .... make sure it was always neat and tidy, as well.

4 Tom: What .... (you) do to get your international driver's licence?

Tina: I .... show the police my Canadian driver's licence, but I .... (not) take another driving test.

5 Matt: Our children enjoyed the summer camp.

Julie: .... (they) help at mealtimes?

Matt: Well, they .... (not) make the food, but they .... (help) with the dishes.

B Complete the sentences with *should have* or *shouldn't have* for these situations.

▶ Pedro didn't take his medicine. Later he got very sick.
  Pedro *should have taken* his medicine.
▶ Sara drove her car when she was tired and she had an accident.
  Sara *shouldn't have driven* her car when she was tired.
1 Aaron didn't buy any sugar so he couldn't make a cake.
  Aaron .... some sugar.
2 Katie had a cold but she still went to the party. Later she had to stay in bed.
  Katie .... to the party.
3 Richard ate a lot of cupcakes. Later he had stomach ache.
  Richard .... so many cupcakes.
4 Lucy didn't lock the door to her apartment when she went to buy a newspaper.
  While she was away, someone stole her television.
  Lucy .... the door when she went out.
5 Mary borrowed Tom's camera without asking him.
  Mary .... Tom's camera without asking him.

C Here is the work plan for the Information Office at Montréal–Mirabel Airport for last weekend. If someone did not in fact work, there is a comment.

SATURDAY		SUNDAY	
On duty	Comments	On duty	Comments
Jenny	✓	Colin	✓
Brian	sick	Marie	✓
Joanne	sick	Derek	sick
Daniel	✓	Carol	sick

From the information in the table, write complete sentences using *had to*, *didn't have to*, or *should have* and the words in parentheses ( ).

▶ (Jenny/Saturday) *Jenny had to work on Saturday.*
▶ (Colin/Saturday) *Colin didn't have to work on Saturday.*
▶ (Carol/Sunday) *Carol should have worked on Sunday* but she was sick.
1 (Colin/Sunday) ....
2 (Joanne/Sunday) ....
3 (Derek/Sunday) .... but he was sick.
4 (Marie/Saturday) ....
5 (Brian/Saturday) .... but he was sick.
6 (Daniel/Saturday) ....
7 (Joanne/Saturday) .... but she was sick.
8 (Derek/Saturday) ....

Passive sentences (1)

1 We form the Simple Present passive like this:

am/is/are	+	PAST PARTICIPLE	
Glass	*is*	*made*	*from sand.*

POSITIVE AND NEGATIVE
*This series **is shown** on TV every Thursday.*
*These computers **aren't produced** any more.*

QUESTIONS
*When **is** breakfast **served** in this hotel?*

(For information on the forms of regular past participles, see Appendix 2, page 95, and for irregular past participles, see Appendix 3, page 96.)

2 We form the Simple Past passive like this:

was/were	+	PAST PARTICIPLE	
Anna	*was*	*born*	*in Germany.*

POSITIVE AND NEGATIVE
Romeo and Juliet *was written* by
  Shakespeare.
*The goods **weren't delivered** yesterday.*

QUESTIONS
*When **was** your camera **stolen**?*

3 Look at these sentences:

ACTIVE: *They sell* | OBJECT |
                    | *cold drinks* | *here.*

PASSIVE: | *Cold drinks* |
         | SUBJECT | *are sold here.*

Notice that the object in the active sentence (**cold drinks**) is the same as the subject in the passive sentence. We use the passive when it is not important who does the action, or when we don't know who does it:
These cars are made in Japan. (We don't need to say ... ~~by Japanese workers~~.)
This house was built in the eighteenth century. (We don't know who built it.)

4 Now look at these examples:
  (i) *Alfred Hitchcock was a great filmmaker. He directed this film in 1956.*
  (ii) *This is a wonderful film. It was directed by Alfred Hitchcock.*

In (ii) we use the passive because we have been talking about something (**the film**), and not the person who did it (**Hitchcock**). We use **by** to say who does, or did, the action:
*This film was directed **by** Hitchcock.*

Practice

A Complete these sentences using the correct form of the verbs from the box. Use the passive form of the Simple Present or Simple Past.

build	check	found	hold	~~make~~	produce	~~fix~~	sell	speak	write

▶ Scotch whiskey is made............. in Scotland.
▶ The car was fixed............ last week.
1 The Winter Olympics .... every four years.
2 English .... in many countries.
3 "Hallelujah" .... by Leonard Cohen.
4 Car speeds .... by radar.
5 The Ambassador Bridge .... to connect Windsor with Detroit.
6 Souvenirs .... at all popular tourist destinations.
7 The first Volkswagen Beetles .... in 1937.
8 The *Montreal Gazette* .... in 1778.

B Now write the questions for the sentences in exercise A, using the passive form.

▶ Where is Scotch whiskey made? ....
▶ When was the car fixed? ....
1 How often ....
2 Where ....
3 Who ....
4 How ....
5 Why ....
6 Where ....
7 When ....
8 When ....

C Change the active sentences into passive sentences. Use the words in parentheses ( ).

▶ We sell tickets for all shows at the box office. (Tickets for all shows/sell/at the box office)
  Tickets for all shows are sold at the box office. ....

1 Thomas Edison invented the electric light bulb. (The electric light bulb/invent/by Thomas Edison)
  ....

2 Someone painted the office last week. (The office/paint/last week)
  ....

3 Several people saw the accident. (The accident/see/by several people)
  ....

4 Where do they make these TVs? (Where/these TVs/make)
  ....

5 Six countries signed the agreement. (The agreement/sign/by six countries)
  ....

6 A stranger helped me. (I/help/by a stranger)
  ....

7 They don't deliver the mail on Sundays. (The mail/not/deliver/on Sundays)
  ....

D Write the correct active or passive form in parentheses ( ).

Fiat (▶) was started .... (started/was started) by a group of Italian businessmen
in 1899. In 1903, Fiat (1)....................... (produced/was produced) 132 cars.
Some of these cars (2)....................... (exported/were exported) by the
company to the United States and Britain. In 1920, Fiat (3).......................
(started/was started) making cars at a new factory at Lingotto, near Turin. There
was a track on the roof where the cars (4)....................... (tested/were tested)
by technicians. In 1936, Fiat launched the Fiat 500. This car (5).......................
(called/was called) the Topolino — the Italian name for Mickey Mouse. The company
grew, and in 1963 Fiat (6)....................... (exported/was exported) more than
300,000 vehicles. Today, Fiat is based in Turin, and its cars (7).......................
(sold/are sold) all over the world.

Passive sentences (2)

1 Here is a summary of the passive voice. Note that we always use a past participle with the passive voice (e.g. **repaired, taken**). For more information on past participles, see Appendices 2 and 3, pages 95–96.

Simple Present:

VERB (present) + PARTICIPLE
ACTIVE: *Someone **repairs** the machine.*
PASSIVE: *The machine **is repaired**.*

Simple Past:

VERB (past) + PARTICIPLE
ACTIVE: *Someone **took** my camera.*
PASSIVE: *My camera **was taken**.*

Present Perfect:

have/has + PARTICIPLE
ACTIVE: *She **has packed** the books.*
PASSIVE: *The books **have been packed**.*

Past Perfect:

had + PARTICIPLE
ACTIVE: *Bob **had paid** the bill.*
PASSIVE: *The bill **had been paid**.*

Present Progressive:

am/is/are + -ing + PARTICIPLE
ACTIVE: *They **are fixding** the car.*
PASSIVE: *The car **is being fixed**.*

Past Progressive:

was/were + -ing + PARTICIPLE
ACTIVE: *They **were building** it.*
PASSIVE: *It **was being built**.*

will, can, must, etc.

+ INFINITIVE + PARTICIPLE
ACTIVE: *We **will finish** the job.*
PASSIVE: *The job **will be finished**.*
ACTIVE: *We **must do** the work.*
PASSIVE: *The work **must be done**.*

2 In all passive sentences, the first verb (= auxiliary verb) is singular if the subject is singular, and plural if the subject is plural:

	AUXILIARY VERB	
The house	*is*	*being built.*
The houses	*are*	*being built.*

We also use the auxiliary verb to make questions and negatives:
Have the books been packed?
*The bill **hadn't** been paid.*

Practice

A Make questions from the passive sentences in parentheses ( ).

▶ (That car was made in Germany.) Where was that car made?
1 (Mary was examined by the doctor this morning.) When ....
2 (The food will be prepared on Friday.) When ....
3 (This window has been broken three times.) How many times ....

B Write the negative of the sentences in exercise A.

▶ That car was not made in Germany. ....
1 Mary ....
2 The food ....
3 This window ....

C Complete the sentences with a passive form of the verb in parentheses ( ).

▶ Bread _is made_.............. (make) from flour.
▶ I was at school when these houses _were being built_..... (was building).
1 Cakes .... (make) from flour.
2 We lived in a hotel while our house .... (was building).
3 This work .... (must finish) before five o'clock.
4 All the windows .... (have cleaned) this week.
5 These cups .... (broke) when we arrived.
6 Some money .... (have stolen) from Tony's jacket.

D Make these active sentences passive. Use a phrase with *by*.

▶ Your manager must write the report.
   The report _must be written by your manager._...
▶ The children are organizing the Christmas party.
   The Christmas party _is being organized by the children._................................
1 The French team has won the silver medal.
   The silver medal ....
2 A woman was training the guard dogs.
   The guard dogs ....
3 People of all ages can play this game.
   This game ....
4 A large crowd was watching the bonspiel.
   The bonspiel ....
5 The prime minister sent a reply.
   A reply ....
6 Two different teachers have marked the tests.
   The tests ....
7 A police car is following that green van.
   That green van ....

E Complete the sentences with the correct passive form of the verb in parentheses ( ).

▶ The castle _was built_............ (build) in 1546.
▶ These mountains can _be seen_.............. (see) from a great distance.
1 These houses .... (build) in 1996.
2 The repairs must .... (finish) by tomorrow.
3 The town has .... (attack) several times since the beginning of the war.
4 The decision has already .... (make).
5 The emails will .... (send) tomorrow morning.
6 White wine can .... (make) from red grapes.
7 The accident happened while the cars .... (load) onto the ferry.
8 The new models will .... (deliver) next week.

Have something done

1 Look at this sentence:

*Marvin and Rose **painted** their apartment.*

This tells us that Marvin and Rose were the painters; they painted their apartment.

Now look at this sentence with **have something done**:

*Jenny and John **had** their apartment **painted**.*

This tells us that Jenny and John wanted their apartment painted, and that someone painted it for them.

2 Here are some more examples:

HAVE	+	SOMETHING	+	DONE
I have fixed		*my bike.*		
I have had		*my bike*		*fixed.*

*Sheila **is going to cut** her hair.*
*Sheila **is going to have** her hair **cut**.*
  (= Someone is going to cut it for her.)
*She **washes** her car every Sunday.*
*She **has** her car **washed** every Sunday.*
  (= Someone washes her car for her.)

*I **must clean** my suit this week.*
*I **must have** my suit **cleaned** this week.*
  (= I must pay someone to clean it for me.)
*I'll **fix** that broken window.*
*I'll **have** that broken window **fixed**.*
  (= Someone will fix that window for me.)

3 We sometimes use **get** instead **of have**:
  *I must **get** my suit **cleaned**.*

4 Now look at this example:

*Susan is very angry. She **had** her bike **stolen**.*

Here, we use **have something done** to talk about something that happens to someone, usually something unpleasant. Here is another example:

*The band **had** two concerts **cancelled** because of bad weather.*

Practice

A Write sentences with a form of *have something done* for these situations. Use the correct tense.

▶ Raul's windows were dirty, but he didn't have time to clean them himself.
Last Saturday, Raul *had his windows cleaned.*

1 The store delivers Mary's food to her house.
Mary ....

2 At the butcher's Fred said, "Please cut the meat into small pieces."
Fred .... into small pieces.

3 The hairdresser cuts Rachel's hair about twice a year.
Rachel .... about twice a year.

4 Last week, the optician checked Mr. Agarwal's eyes.
Last week, Mr. Agarwal ....

5 Mrs. Zhang's doctor says to her: "When you come to see me next week, I'll check your blood pressure."
When Mrs. Zhang goes to see the doctor next week, she ....

6 Last week, the mechanic serviced Jane's car.
Last week, Jane ....

7 A builder is going to fix the roof on our house.
We .... on our house.

B Look at these signs from some businesses. Then write what people think when they see the signs, using the words in parentheses ( ) and *have* or *had*.

▶ WE REPAIR ALL KINDS OF BOOTS AND SHOES
(That reminds me. I/must/my brown boots/repair)
That reminds me. *I must have my brown boots repaired.*

1 LET US CLEAN YOUR CARPETS AND CURTAINS
(My parents use that company. They/their carpets/clean/there)
My parents use that company. ....

2 CAN WE CHECK YOUR OIL AND TIRES?
(That reminds me. I/must/the tires/check)
That reminds me. ....

3 WE MAKE ALL TYPES OF KEYS
(I'd almost forgotten. I/ought to/a new key/make/for the front door)
I'd almost forgotten. ....

4 OUR SPECIALITY: PAINTING HOUSES AND APARTMENTS
(I don't think I can afford to/our apartment/paint)
I don't think I can afford to ....

5 WE FIX WATCHES AND CLOCKS
(That store isn't expensive. I/my watch/fix/there last week)
That store isn't expensive. ....

6 WE TEST YOUR EYES FOR FREE
(Ah, yes! My husband/his eyes/test/there last winter)
Ah, yes! ....

7 WE REMOVE ALL KINDS OF STAINS FROM ALL KINDS OF CLOTHES
(Wonderful! I'll take my suit there and/that coffee stain/remove)
Wonderful! I'll take my suit there and I'll ....

C Some unpleasant things happened to these people last week. Use the sentence in parentheses ( ) to write a sentence with *had something done*.

▶ (Vera's purse was pulled off her shoulder.)
Vera *had her purse pulled off her shoulder.*

1 (Peter's driver's licence was taken away by the police.)
Peter ....

2 (Paula's bike was stolen from the garage.)
Paula ....

3 (Fiona's glasses were broken.)
....

4 (John's clothes were torn in a fight.)
....

5 (Jane's apartment was robbed on the weekend.)
....

6 (Our electricity was cut off because we had forgotten to pay the bill.)
....

Verb + **to** or verb + **-ing**

1 Look at these sentences:
> My sister **promised to help** me.
> John doesn't **want to wait**.

We use **to** + **infinitive** after some verbs, e.g.:

afford	dare	decide	
deserve	want	hope	
learn	mean	offer	**+ to +**
pretend	promise	refuse	INFINITIVE
seem	plan	agree	
arrange	have (="must")		

2 Look at these sentences:
> Have they **finished painting** the garage?
> We **enjoy sitting** on the balcony.

We use an **-ing** form after other verbs, e.g.:

avoid	dislike	enjoy	
finish	give up	imagine	**+ -ing**
keep	practise	stop	

3 Look at these sentences:
> Jenny **likes to stay** at home.
> Jenny **likes staying** at home.

These verbs can usually take an **-ing** form or **to** + **infinitive** with no difference in meaning:

begin	continue	hate	intend
like	love	prefer	start

But after **would hate, would like, would love** or **would prefer**, we use **to** + **infinitive**:
> **Would** you like to go for a walk?
> I'**d love to visit** Australia.

4 We can use an **-ing** form or **to** + **infinitive** after these verbs, but the meaning is different:

try	remember	forget

► *I **tried to lift that** heavy rock.* (= make an attempt: I made an attempt to lift the rock.)
*If you can't read where you are, **try sitting** nearer the window.* (= Test something out: sit nearer the window and see if you can read there.)

► *Remember to go to the bank.* (= Remember that you must go to the bank.)
*She **remembers going to** the bank.* (= She remembers that she went to the bank.)

► *Don't **forget to call** Ms. Ruiz.* (= Remember that you must call Ms. Ruiz.)
*I'll never **forget seeing** that meteor shower.* (= I saw that meteor shower, and I'll always remember it.)

Practice

A Write the correct form of the verb in parentheses ( ).

► Paul dared <u>to argue</u> (argue) with the police.
► I can't imagine <u>living</u> (live) in the country.
1 We've decided .... (go) to the beach.
2 I stopped .... (play) rugby when I got married.
3 I meant .... (buy) some butter, but I forgot.
4 Did you promise .... (take) the children to Banff?
5 Have the men finished .... (fix) the roof yet?
6 I'd love .... (visit) China.
7 You shouldn't avoid .... (talk) about your problems.
8 Peter refused .... (help) us.
9 Would you prefer .... (pay) now or later?
10 I couldn't afford .... (live) in Toronto.
11 Why does Eric keep .... (talk) about his mother?

B Complete this conversation between Janet and Sharon with the correct form of the verbs in parentheses ( ).

Janet: What do your children (▶) <u>want to do</u>......... (want/do) when they finish school?

Sharon: Well, Ann (▶) <u>enjoys writing</u>....... (enjoy/write), so she's (▶) <u>hoping to work</u>...... (hope/work) for a newspaper. But I don't know about Malcolm. He (1)...................... (give up/study) months ago. He seems to (2)...................... (enjoy/do) nothing now. He doesn't (3)...................... (deserve/pass) his exams. And he (4)...................... (refuse/listen) to us, when we tell him to (5)...................... (keep/study).

Janet: With our children, in the past, if we (6)...................... (offer/help) them, they always (7)...................... (promise/study) hard. Nowadays if they (8)...................... (want/talk) to us, that's fine, but I've learned to (9)...................... (stop/ask) them questions. I suppose they (10)...................... (dislike/listen) to my suggestions. They (11)...................... (seem/think) that they don't (12)...................... (need/study) hard, but one day they'll (13)...................... (have/find) a job.

C Use an *-ing* form, or *to + infinitive*, of the word in parentheses ( ) to complete each sentence.

▶ You say that I've met Malika, but I can't remember her.
   I can't remember <u>meeting</u>...... (meet) Malika.

1 Please remember that you must buy some stamps.
   Please remember .... (buy) some stamps.

2 We wanted to open the door, but we couldn't.
   We tried .... (open) the door.

3 Jonah met Madonna once. He'll never forget it.
   Jonah will never forget .... (meet) Madonna.

4 Stella intended to call Dwight, but she forgot.
   Stella forgot .... (call) Dwight.

5 Jenny had a headache. She took a pain reliever, but it didn't help.
   Jenny tried .... (take) a pain reliever for her headache.

6 I have a special soap that will probably get your hands clean.
   Try .... (wash) your hands with this special soap.

7 It will not be easy to do all the work today.
   We'll try .... (finish) the work before tonight.

8 I stayed in Jane's apartment while she was on vacation. I remembered that I had to feed her cats every day.
   I remembered .... (feed) Jane's cats every day while she was on vacation.

9 Remember that you must invite Toni to the party next week.
   Don't forget .... (invite) Toni to the party next week.

Purpose: for ...ing

1 Read this dialogue:
   A: *What's this machine for?*
   B: *It's for cutting cloth.*

The question **What is it for?** asks about the purpose of something (what we use something for). When we describe the purpose of a thing, we use **for + -ing**. Here are some more examples:
   This is an instrument for measuring wind speed.
   This tool is used for making holes.

2 Now look at this dialogue:
   A: *What does he need my camera for?*
      (= Why does he need my camera?)
   B: *He needs it for his work.* (= His work is the reason why he needs the camera.)

The question **What ... for?** asks about purpose. To talk about someone's purpose, we can use **for + noun**. Here are some more examples:
   A: *What did he go to the market for?*
   B: *He went to the market for some fruit.*
      (He wanted to buy some fruit.)

I buy the newspaper for the sports section.
   (= ... in order to read the sports section.)

3 Now look at this dialogue:
   A: *What does he need my camera for?*
   B: *He needs it to take some photos.*
      (= ... in order to take some photos.)

To talk about someone's purpose, we can also use **to + infinitive** (e.g. **to take**). Here are some more examples:
   He went to the market to buy some fruit.
      (= ... in order to buy some fruit.)

John called the police to tell them about the burglar.

Practice

A Write definitions of the things in box A using the phrases from box B.

A
telescope — instrument
~~hammer — tool~~
fridge — appliance
kettle — appliance
thermometer — instrument
vacuum cleaner — appliance
drill — tool
speedometer — instrument
freezer — appliance

B
boil water
measure temperature
~~tap in nails~~
clean carpets
see things at a distance
keep food cold
measure speed
keep food frozen
make holes

▶ A hammer is a tool for tapping in nails.
1 A kettle ....
2 A thermometer ....
3 A vacuum cleaner ....
4 A fridge ....
5 A telescope ....
6 A speedometer ....
7 A freezer ....
8 A drill ....

B In the following short dialogues, use *What ... for?* to write questions using the words in parentheses ( ). Then write a reply using the words in parentheses and *for*.

▶ A: (/did/Meredith/go/to the park/?) *What did Meredith go to the park for?*
  B: (She/go/to the park/some fresh air.) *She went to the park for some fresh air.*

1 A: (/does/Khalid/want/the money/?) ....
  B: (He/want/the money/a train ticket.) ....

2 A: (/does/Philip/want/the flour/?) ....
  B: (He/want/the flour/a cake.) ....

3 A: (/did/Bill/go/to the butcher's/?) ....
  B: (He/go/to the butcher's/some sausages.) ....

4 A: (/does/Helen/want/the polish/?) ....
  B: (She/want/it/her shoes.) ....

5 A: (/did/Alison/go/to the library/?) ....
  B: (She/go/to the library/a book on India.) ....

6 A: (/did/Jane/call/Ann/?) ....
  B: (She/call/Ann/some advice.) ....

C Now write the answers from exercise B using the verbs in the box, as in the example. Use each verb once.

borrow	buy (x2)	clean	get (x2)	make

▶ Meredith: *She went to the park to get some fresh air.*
1 Khalid: ....
2 Philip: ....
3 Bill: ....
4 Helen: ....
5 Alison: ....
6 Jane: ....

D Find the errors and rewrite the sentences correctly.

▶ This machine is for make pasta. *This machine is for making pasta.*
1 For what did he come? ....
2 A bus is for carry passengers. ....
3 She went to the post office for to buy some stamps.
  ....
4 The mayor came for give out the prizes. ....
5 The woman jumped into the river to saving the child.
  ....
6 I'm training hard for to get in shape. ....
7 This is a computer program for make three-dimensional drawings.
  ....
8 Can I use your pen for signing this letter? ....

Verb + object (+ **to**) + infinitive

1 Look at these examples:

> Phyllis said to Bob:
> "*Make some coffee, please.*"
> We can say:
> Phyllis **asked Bob to make** some coffee.

> Ann said to Rose:
> "*Can you come to my party, Rose?*"
> We can say:
> Ann **invited Rose to come** to her party.

> Violetta thinks Chris should see a doctor.
> She can say:
> *I'll* **persuade Chris to go** to the doctor's.

The structure is:

VERB	+ OBJECT	+ **to**	+ INFINITIVE
She asked	*Jill*	*to*	*wait.*
She asked	*her*	*to*	*wait.*

We use these verbs in this structure:

tell	force	teach	
help	allow	would like	
ask	invite	encourage	+ OBJECT + to
want	forbid	persuade	
advise	remind	convince	

2 Note that the first verb can change its tense, but the second verb is always **to** + **infinitive** (**to make**):

> She **is asking Bob** ⎫
> She **will ask Bob** ⎬ *to make some coffee.*
> She **has asked Bob** ⎭

Note that if we use a pronoun, we use **me, him, her, it, us, you, them** (object pronouns) after the verb:

> Phyllis asked **him** to make some coffee.

3 Now look at these two sentences:

> The teacher **let Jane leave** school early.
> I **made him tell** me the truth.

Let here means "allow," and **make** means "force" or "order." **Make** and **let** are followed by an infinitive (without **to**):

	VERB	+ OBJECT	+ INFINITIVE
She	*let*	*Jane*	*leave.*

Feel, hear, see, and **watch** can also be followed by an infinitive (without **to**):

> I **heard** your sister **shout** "Fire!"
> (NOT … ~~to shout~~ …)
> Wayne **saw** a car **come** round the corner.

Practice

A Write complete sentences using the words in parentheses ( ). Be careful to use the correct tense.

▶ (Tomorrow/I/encourage/Janet/enter/the competition.)
  Tomorrow I will encourage Janet to enter the competition.

▶ (I was already tired, but I/force/myself/go on working.)
  I was already tired, but I forced myself to go on working.

1 (Ann/teach/Jorge/drive/last year.)

  ....

2 (Don't worry! Tomorrow I/persuade/my father/see/a doctor.)

  ....

3 (The boss has/forbid/his staff/wear/jeans in the office.)

  ....

4 (Last Sunday, Yan/invite/Sheila/come/for lunch.)

  ....

5 (Next year the teachers/allow/the students/use/calculators during tests.)

  ....

B Use the words in parentheses ( ) to complete the sentences.

▶ (Police officer: "Can everyone please stay indoors?")
The police officer asked everyone <u>to stay indoors.</u>

1 (Keshia: "Remember to come home early, Tim.")
Keshia reminded Tim ....

2 (Manager: "You must work more quickly.")
The boss wants us ....

3 (Captain: "Let's do our best in the game.")
The captain encouraged us ....

4 (Jo: "Can you come to my party next Saturday?")
Jo invited me ....

C Answer the questions, changing the nouns (e.g. *Michael*) to pronouns (e.g. *him*).
Be careful to use the correct tense.

▶ A: Did Nicola tell Michael to be careful?
B: Yes, <u>she told him to be careful.</u>

1 A: Would Kate like Peter to stay?
B: Yes, ...

2 A: Did Mrs. Slater help her son to finish?
B: Yes, ...

3 A: Did the doctor advise Raphael to stay in bed?
B: Yes, ...

4 A: Does Lisa allow her children to go to late-night parties?
B: Yes, ...

5 A: Did Ann-Marie remind Mark to call?
B: Yes, ...

D Write a sentence with a similar meaning, using the verb in parentheses ( ).

▶ The police told everyone to leave the building.
(make) <u>The police made everyone leave the building.</u>

1 The driver allowed the elderly man to travel on the bus without a ticket.
(let) ....

2 Jack told his younger brother to wash the dishes.
(make) ....

3 I don't allow people to smoke in my house or in my car!
(let) ....

E Combine the two sentences into one.

▶ Your sister shouted "Fire!" I heard her.
<u>I heard your sister shout "Fire!"</u>

1 Thomas made the sandwiches. Aestus watched him.
Aestus ....

2 The ground shook. We felt it.
We ....

3 Brian left early. Did you see him?
Did you ....

What ... like?

1 Look at this question and answer:
   A: **What's** Julie **like**?
   B: *She's very pretty and she's very kind, but she's not very smart.*

We use **What ... like?** to ask about a person's physical appearance (tall, short, pretty, etc.) or character (interesting, boring, friendly, unfriendly, etc).

We can also use **What ... like?** to ask about places, books, movies, and events (e.g. a party, a football game):
   A: **What's** Rio de Janeiro **like**?
   B: *Well, the beaches are wonderful but the traffic is awful.*
   A: **What's** Burton's latest movie **like**?
   B: *It's excellent.*

2 We use **look like?** to talk about someone's appearance:
   A: **What** does Julie **look like**?
   B: *She's tall with brown hair.*

We can also use **like** with **taste, feel, sound,** and **smell**:
   A: **What** does that **taste like**?
   B: *It **tastes like** cheese.*

A: *What is this material?*
B: *I don't know. It **looks like** wool but it **feels like** cotton.*

3 We can also use **like**, with the question word **Who** and in statements, to mean "similar to":
   A: **Who's** Julie **like** – her father or her mother?
   B: *She's **like** her mother. (= She is similar to her mother.)*
   *Rio de Janeiro is **like** Buenos Aires. (= Rio is similar to Buenos Aires.)*

4 The word **like** in **What's she like?** is a preposition; it is not the verb **like**. Here is an example of **like** used as a verb:
   A: *What music does Julie **like**?*
   B: *She **likes** jazz music.*

5 We usually use **How?**, not **What ... like?**, when we ask about someone's health or temporary state:
   A: **How's** your brother today?
   B: *He's feeling much better.*
   A: **How** was your boss today?
   B: *He was very friendly today!*

Practice

A Use the words in parentheses ( ) to write a question that goes with the answer. Use *is/are* or *look*. Sometimes more than one answer is possible.

▶ (What/Alix/like)
   A: <u>What is Alix like</u> ?   ~ B: She's smart, but she's a bit boring.

▶ (What/Jaclyn/like)
   A: <u>What does Jaclyn look like</u> ?   ~ B: She's short and has dark hair.

1 (What/Josiah/like)
   A: .... ?   ~ B: He's not a very interesting person.

2 (What/Angie's parents/like)
   A: .... ?   ~ B: They're very generous.

3 (What/Stuart/like)
   A: .... ?   ~ B: He's very tall, and he has blond hair.

4 (What/Katie/like)
   A: .... ?   ~ B: She's tall and strong.

5 (What/Bob and Mike/like)
   A: .... ?   ~ B: They're very amusing.

6 (What/Shannon/like)
   A: .... ?   ~ B: She's tall and slim, and she wears glasses.

B Read the following descriptions.

Kiwis are a round, brown fruit with a rough skin. They have almost no smell, but they are sweet, with a flavour similar to strawberries.
A double bass is a musical instrument. It is the largest member of the violin family. It has a deep sound.

Now for each of the answers, write a question about kiwis or a double bass, using *look/sound/taste/smell/feel* + *like*.

QUESTION	ANSWER
▶ What do kiwis look like ....?	~ They're round and brown.
1 ....?	~ It has a deep sound.
2 ....?	~ They don't really have a smell.
3 ....?	~ They have a flavour like strawberries.
4 ....?	~ Like a very big violin.
5 ....?	~ They are rough to the touch.

C Use the words in parentheses ( ) to write a question with the preposition *like* or the verb *like*. Add any other necessary words.

▶ (What music/you/like)
A: What music do you like ....? ~ B: I like bluegrass music.

▶ (What/Julie/like)
A: What is Julie like ....? ~ B: She is very amusing.

1 (Who/your sister/like)
A: ....? ~ B: She likes a boy in her class.

2 (What/Paul's brothers/like)
A: ....? ~ B: They think they're smart, but I don't.

3 (What/Rachel/like/for breakfast)
A: ....? ~ B: She likes bacon and eggs.

4 (Who/you/like)
A: ....? ~ B: I'm like my mother.

5 (What/Marie's husband/like)
A: ....? ~ B: He is a bit boring. He's not like her.

D Write questions with *What ... like?* (for things that are permanent) or *How ... ?* (for health or temporary situations). Use a form of *be* and the other words in parentheses ( ).

▶ (be/Vancouver) What is Vancouver like ....? ~ It's a very lively city.
▶ (be/Todd/yesterday) How was Todd yesterday.. ? ~ He felt a lot better.
1 (be/Hudson's apartment) ....? ~ It's very big, and it has a wonderful view over the city.

2 (be/your boss/yesterday)..............................? ~ He was tired but friendly.
3 (be/a squash racquet)..............................? ~ It's similar to a tennis racquet, but lighter.

4 (be/your sister)..............................? ~ She's very well, thank you.
5 (be/Portugal)..............................? ~ It's very interesting. There are lots of things to see.

Reported speech (1)

1 When we report something that somebody said, we usually change the tense of the verb like this:

ACTUAL WORDS	REPORTED SPEECH
Simple Present *"I live in a small apartment,"* she said.	→ Simple Past *She said she lived in a small apartment.*
Present Progressive *"I'm leaving on Tuesday,"* I said.	→ Past Progressive *I said that I was leaving on Tuesday.*
Simple Past Present Perfect } *"I learned a lot,"* he said. *"Mr. Jackson has left,"* she said.	→ Past Perfect *He said he had learned a lot.* *She said that Mr. Jackson had left.*
will *"I'll help you,"* she said.	→ would *She said she would help me.*
am/is/are going to *"We're going to be late,"* I said.	→ was/were going to *I said that we were going to be late.*
can *"I can't find my money,"* he said.	→ could *He said he couldn't find his money.*

2 Note that it is not necessary to use **that** in reported speech:
> *She said (**that**) she knew the answer.*

3 Compare **say** and **tell** in these sentences:
> *She **said** (that) she lived in a small apartment.*
> *She **told me** (that) she lived in a small apartment.*

We **say something.** We do not **say someone something.**
> *She said she was going to be late.*
> (NOT ~~She said me she was…~~)
> *I said that I disagreed with him.*
> (NOT ~~I said him that I…~~)

We **tell someone something.** We do not **tell something.**
> *He told **me** he was happy.*
> (NOT ~~He told he was happy.~~)
> *He told **me** that he would pay me immediately.*
> (NOT ~~He told that he would pay me immediately.~~)
> *She told **Fred** she was going to meet someone.*
> (NOT ~~She told that she was going to meet someone.~~)

Practice

A Look at these pictures of people coming through passport control at an airport. Change the things they said into reported speech.

I am visiting friends. — I am going to a conference. — I have lost my passport. — We have been on holiday. — I don't understand.

▶ He said *that he was visiting friends.*

1 She said ....

2 He said ....

3 They said ....

4 She said ....

B Read this conversation and then report what Claudia and Nicole said.

Nicole: How long have you been in France?
Claudia: Six weeks.
Nicole: Are you enjoying your stay?
Claudia: Yes, I'm enjoying it a lot.
Nicole: Have you been here before?
Claudia: Yes. I've been to France many times.
Nicole: What are you doing here?
Claudia: I'm on vacation.
Nicole: Are you staying in a hotel?
Claudia: No, I'm staying with some friends.
Nicole: Where do they live?
Claudia: They have an apartment in Paris.
Nicole: How long are you staying?
Claudia: I'm leaving in March.
Nicole: Can you speak French very well?
Claudia: No, I can't. I'm going to take some lessons.
Nicole: I'll teach you.

▶ Claudia said (that) she had been .... in France for six weeks.
1 Claudia said .... her stay a lot.
2 Claudia said .... to France many times.
3 Claudia said .... on vacation.
4 She said .... with some friends.
5 She said .... an apartment in Paris.
6 She said .... in March.
7 She said .... French very well.
8 She said .... some lessons.
9 Nicole said .... Claudia.

C Complete the sentences with *said* or *told*.

▶ She said .... she wasn't feeling very well.
1 Alex .... me that he would buy the tickets.
2 They .... that the train was going to be late.
3 She .... him that she was very angry with him.
4 She .... him that she couldn't help him.
5 Who .... you that I was leaving? It's not true!
6 They .... us that they were leaving in the morning.
7 He .... that he didn't know what was wrong with the car.
8 She .... she had four sisters.
9 She .... me that Tom worked in a factory.
10 He .... me that he was a doctor, but he .... Anna that he was
a dentist.

Reported speech (2)

1 REQUESTS

There are different ways to make a request, e.g.:

Sarah: *"Please wait a minute, Tom."*
Sarah: *"Will you wait a minute, please?"*
Sarah: *"Tom, could you wait a minute, please?"*

We can report all of these requests in the same way, using **asked**:

*Sarah **asked** Tom to wait a minute.*

We do not usually use **please** in a reported question.

2 ORDERS

There are different ways to give an order:

"Stand up, John."
"You must work harder."

We can report orders like this, using **told**:

*He **told** John to stand up.*
*He **told** me to work harder.*

3 ADVICE

We can give advice like this:

"You should get married, Aaron."
"You should stop smoking, Crystal."

We can report advice like this, using **advised**:

*He **advised** Aaron to get married.*
*He **advised** Crystal to stop smoking.*

4 In reported speech, we use **ask**, **tell**, and **advise** like this:

	VERB +	OBJECT +	to + INFINITIVE
Sarah	asked	Tom	to wait.
She	told	him	to stand.
He	advised	Crystal	to stop smoking.

Here is a list of common verbs that we use in this structure:

advise	ask	tell	order
persuade	remind	forbid	warn

Examples:

I'll remind them to come early.
I advised them to go to the police.

We cannot use **say** in this structure:

She said (that) he should wait.
(NOT ~~She said him to wait.~~)

5 To report a negative request, order, etc. (e.g. *"Don't laugh"*), we use **not + to + infinitive**:

	VERB +	OBJECT +	not + to + INFINITIVE
Jay	told	Tom	not to laugh.
They	warned	Ian	not to borrow money.
I	reminded	John	not to be late.

Practice

A Rewrite the sentences using an *object + to + infinitive*, as in the example.

▶ "Make some coffee please, Bob."
Kumar asked <u>Bob to make some coffee.</u>

1 "You must do the homework soon, Jane."
She told ....

2 "Remember to buy a map, Ann."
He reminded ....

3 "You should see a doctor, Mrs. Clark."
He advised ....

4 "Keep all the windows closed, Bill."
They warned ....

5 "Go home, Paul."
Francis told ....

B Report what these people said using the words in parentheses ( ). Use the Simple Past.

▶ Fred said, "Milos, would you lend me five dollars, please?"
(ask) Fred asked Milos to lend him five dollars. ....

1 I said to Frederique, "Remember to call Sally."
(remind) ....

2 "You must wash your hands, children," the teacher said.
(tell) ....

3 "Jessica, please lend me your bicycle pump," said Paul.
(ask) ....

4 She said, "Children, stay away from the water."
(warn) ....

5 "You should see a lawyer," the police officer said to Maurice.
(advise) ....

C Complete the conversations using the words in parentheses ( ). You will also need a pronoun (e.g. *me, him, them*) and the word *not*. Use the Simple Past.

▶ A: Did you tell the children to wash the car?   B: (Yes, but I/tell/to use too much water.)
B: Yes, but I told them not to use too much water. ....

1 A: Did you ask Steve to come to the meeting?   B: (Yes, and I/tell/to be late.)
B: ....

2 A: Did the doctor tell Jodi to keep warm?   B: (Yes, and she/warn/to go outside the house.)
B: ....

3 A: Did you ask Michael to mail the letters?   B: (Yes, and I/tell/to forget the stamps.)
B: ....

4 A: Did the police officer advise everyone to stay indoors?   B: (Yes, and he/tell/to go near the windows.)
B: ....

5 A: Did the dentist advise you to eat carefully?   B: (Yes, and she specifically/warn/to eat nuts.)
B: ....

D Complete the sentences using the words in the box. Use each word once.

advise	ask	order	remind	~~tell~~	warn

▶ The woman said to Gerald, "Go to Room 23." The woman told him to go .... to Room 23.

1 "Girls, you must not touch these wires. They could be dangerous," said the guide.
The guide .... the wires.

2 "The bus is all right, Annabelle, but it's better for you to take the train," we said.
We .... the train.

3 "Bring the money, Simon. Don't forget," Mrs. Khan said.
Mrs. Khan .... the money.

4 "This is the police," the voice said. "Spectators must leave immediately."
The police .... at once.

5 I said, "Please come in, Mr. Tremblay." I .... in.

Reported questions

1 "Yes/no" questions have a form of **be** (e.g. **is**, **are**) or an auxiliary verb (e.g. **can**, **do**, **have**) that goes before the subject:

	SUBJECT	
"Are	*they*	*Canadian?"*
"Can	*Jules*	*ski?"*

We report these questions with **ask if/ whether**:

	SUBJECT	
*She asked **if***	*they*	*were Canadian.*
*She asked **if***	*Jules*	*could ski.*

or:

*She asked **whether** they **were** Canadian.*
*She asked **whether** Jules **could** ski.*

Note that in a reported question we do not put **be** or an auxiliary before the subject (NOT ~~She asked were they Canadian.~~)

2 Many questions begin with a question word (**Who**, **What**, **Where**, etc.):

	SUBJECT	
"Where does	*Ariel*	*live?"*
"Why has	*Jen*	*gone away?"*

We report these questions with **ask**:

	SUBJECT	
*They asked **where***	*Ariel*	*lived.*
*She asked **why***	*Jen*	*had gone away.*

3 We can also **ask someone something**:
*The manager asked **me** if I could speak French.*
*They asked **him** where Sarah lived.*

4 Note that when we report a question that somebody asked, we usually change the tense of the verb:
"Can Miguel skate?"
*He asked if Miguel **could** skate.*

The most common tense changes are:

▶ Present → Past:
am/is → was   are → were
is living → was living   live → lived

▶ Present Perfect → Past Perfect:
has gone → had gone

▶ Simple Past → Past Perfect:
arrived → had arrived

▶ Modals:
will → would   can → could

We often also change other words, for example:
*"Have **you** finished, Mike?"*
*She asked Mike if **he** had finished.*

5 We can use **wanted to know** and **wondered** instead of **asked**:
*She **wanted to know** if they were Canadian.*
*(OR She wanted to know **whether** they were Canadian.)*
*She **wondered** why Jen had gone away.*

Practice

A Change each sentence into reported speech or a direct question by filling in the blanks. End each sentence with a period (.) or a question mark (?).

▶ (Did they come?) She asked *if*............... they had come.........

▶ (I asked him where he worked.) *Where*.......... do you work.?......

1 (Do you speak English?) They asked me .... I spoke English ....

2 (I wanted to know why he had taken my key.) .... did you take my key........

3 (How many people went to the party?) I asked .... people had gone to the party........

4 (Does Kevin work on Saturdays?) I asked .... Kevin worked on Saturdays........

5 (Can we meet tomorrow?) I asked .... we could meet tomorrow........

6 (I asked what he had done.) .... has he done........

7 (Was Evan born in 1995 or 1996?) I asked them .... Evan was born........
8 (Why has Jane gone home?) I asked .... Jane had gone home........
9 (Where do you go for your vacations?) I wanted to know .... they went for their
   vacations........
10 (Is Scott coming to the party, Athena?) I asked Athena .... Scott was coming to
   the party........

B **Use the words in parentheses ( ) to write a question, and then complete the reported question.**

▶ (Where/have/Maria/go/?) Question: <u>Where has Maria gone?</u>............................
   Reported question: I asked <u>where Maria had gone.</u>................................
1 (Do/Jim/often/play/football/?) Question: ....
   Reported question: I wondered if ....
2 (What/have/the children/eat/?) Question: ....
   Reported question: She wanted to know ....
3 (Where/be/Mark/going/?) Question: ....
   Reported question: I asked ....
4 (When/be/the next bus/?) Question: ....
   Reported question: We wanted to know ....
5 (Have/Ann/see/this movie/?) Question: ....
   Reported question: Tom asked ....

C **Steven Ellis robbed a bank. The police believe that Alain Hebert helped him. A police officer asked Hebert these questions:**

▶ How long have you been out of prison?	
1 Have you worked since then?	4 Do you know Steven Ellis?
2 Does your sister give you money?	5 How long have you known Steven?
3 Who else gives you money?	6 Have you seen Steven recently?

Later the police officer talked about the interview. Complete what she said, using the questions in the box.

▶ I asked him <u>how long he had been out of prison</u>..................., and he replied
   that he had gotten out of prison six months ago.
1 Then I asked him .... He told me that he
   hadn't found a job.
2 I asked him ...., and he said she did give
   him some money, but not very much.
3 Then I asked him .... He replied that
   nobody else did.
4 I asked him ...., and he said that he and
   Steven were friends.
5 So I asked him .... and he said that he
   had known him for six years.
6 Then I asked him ...., and he said that
   he couldn't remember.

Articles: **a/an**, **the**, or no article

1 We use **a/an** with singular nouns:
*He was reading **a book.***
*I saw **an interesting movie** yesterday.*

2 Look at this example:
*When I arrived, John was reading **a book.***

We use **a/an** when it isn't necessary to make clear which specific thing we are talking about. There are lots of books; John was reading one of them.

We use **a/an** to talk about people's jobs:
*Jim is **an engineer.*** (= There are lots of engineers; Jim is one.)

We use **a/an** to describe things or people:
*They have **a beautiful house.*** (= There are lots of beautiful houses; they have one.)
*John is **an old friend** of mine.*

3 We use **the** with singular or plural nouns:
the book   the books

We can use **the** with uncountable nouns (e.g. **music, water, food, snow**):
***The water** is in the fridge.*

Note:

▶ uncountable nouns do not have a plural (NOT ~~two musics, three waters~~).

▶ we do not use **a/an** with uncountable nouns (NOT ~~a music, a water~~).

4 We use **the** when it is clear which person or thing we are talking about:
*Karen was reading **a book**. She closed **the book**.* (= She closed the book that she was reading.)
*Anna likes music, but she doesn't like **the music** that John plays.*
*Mike's gone to **the mall**.* (= the local mall)
*She's in **the kitchen**.* (= the kitchen in this house)
*I must go to **the bank**.* (= my bank, where I keep my money)
the bus station/the airport (in a city)
the Fraser River (There is only one.)
the government in my country

5 We do not use **the** before plural nouns (e.g. **vegetables**) or uncountable nouns (e.g. **education, music**) when we are talking about something in general:
*Do you like **vegetables**?* (= any vegetables)
*I think **education** is very important.*

6 We do not use **a** or **the** before names of languages, meal names, the names of cities, most countries and most streets, and the names of airports, stations, single mountains, or lakes:
*She speaks **Spanish**.*
*She lives in **Amsterdam**, in **Holland**.* (But we say **the** United States, **the** European Union.)
*What time will **lunch** be?*
*from **Mount Lucania** to **Kluane Lake***

Practice

A Write *a*, *an*, or *the* in the blanks if they are required. Leave the blank empty if nothing is required.

▶ I want to put some money into my bank account, so I'm going to <u>the</u>............ bank this afternoon. It's on King Street.

1 I had .... sandwich for .... lunch today.

2 We flew to .... Abbotsford Airport in .... British Columbia.

3 It was .... long flight, but eventually we arrived in .... Panama.

4 I'm trying to learn .... Japanese. I'm taking .... lesson tomorrow.

5 He made .... angry speech against .... government.

6 She is .... famous actress and she is starring in .... popular TV series.

7 They live in .... Paris in .... area near .... River Seine.

8 They bought .... small apartment on .... Victoria Street.

B Complete the sentences by writing *a*, *an*, or *the* if required. Leave the blank empty if nothing is required. (Note that the following words in this exercise are uncountable nouns: *music, gas, education, fish, food, coffee, exercise*.)

▶ She read _the_.... emails she had received that morning.

1 It was a nice day, so we had .... lunch in .... backyard.
2 I'm just going to .... store. I'll be back in a few minutes.
3 We called for .... taxi to take us to .... airport.
4 I like listening to .... music when I come home.
5 Without .... gas or other fuel, ... cars don't work.
6 John was at home. He was reading .... magazine in .... living room.
7 His parents believe that .... education is a very important thing.
8 Jane doesn't like .... fish; she never eats it.
9 After .... dinner, I washed .... plates and glasses.
10 Did you like .... food at .... party yesterday?
11 A: Where's .... coffee?
   B: It's in .... cupboard next to .... sink.
12 Doctors say that .... exercise is good for everybody.

C Complete this conversation by writing *a*, *an*, or *the* if required. Leave the blank empty if nothing is required.

Mike: Is Maria (▶) _a_...... student at your college?
Rosie: No, she's (1)........ old friend of mine. We were in school together.
Mike: What does she do now?
Rosie: She's (2)........ computer programmer. She's not Canadian, you know. She comes from (3)........ Brazil, but she's living in (4)........ US at the moment.
Mike: Has she got (5)........ job there?
Rosie: Yes, she's working for (6)........ big company there.
Mike: Do you send (7)........ emails to each other?
Rosie: Yes, and I had (8)........ long email from her yesterday.
Mike: What did she say in (9)........ email?
Rosie: She said that she was living in (10)........ nice apartment in (11)........ middle of (12)........ Chicago.

D Complete the story by writing *a*, *an*, or *the* in the blanks.

Yesterday I was sitting on (▶) _the_.... six o'clock train when I saw (1)........ strange man walking along the platform. He came into the car of (2)........ train where I was sitting, and he sat in the seat opposite mine. He opened (3)........ newspaper and started reading it. On (4)........ front page of (5)........ newspaper, there was (6)........ picture of (7)........ bank robber. The words under (8)........ picture were: "Wanted by the police." It was (9)........ same man!

There or it/they

1 Look at these sentences:
> *There is a big market near the river; **it is** very good for fruit and meat.*
> *There are two buses on Sunday; **they** both go to the train station.*

We use **there is/are** when we talk about something for the first time in a conversation, and when we say where it is or when it is. We do not use **there** to talk about the same thing again; we use singular **it** (here meaning "the big market") or plural **they** (here meaning "the two buses"). Here are some more examples:
> *There are two schools here; **they** are both new.*
> *There's a good show on Sunday; **it** reports all the sports news.*

2 We use **there** with different forms of **be**:
> *There weren't any CDs forty years ago.*
> A: *Have there been any problems this year?*
> B: *Yes, there have.*
> *There used to be a park here.* (= There was a park here but it isn't here now.)
> *There may be some eggs in the fridge.* (= It is possible that there are some eggs …)

3 We also use **there is/are** etc. to talk about the number of people or things in a place. Look at these questions and answers:
> A: *How many people **were there** at your party?*
> B: *There were about twelve.*
> (NOT ~~We were about twelve.~~)
> A: *Are there many restaurants here?*
> B: *Yes, there must be ten or more.*
> (NOT ~~They must be ten.~~)

We can use **of us, of them**, etc. after the number:
> *There were about twelve **of us**.*

4 For the weather, we use **it** with a verb or adjective, but **there** with a noun:

> **it + verb:** It *snowed* a lot last winter.
> **it + adjective:** It was *foggy/sunny/windy/cloudy*.
> **there + noun:** There was a lot of *fog/wind*.

5 Notice these examples with **it takes**:
> *It takes seven years to become a doctor.*
> A: *How long **does it take** to make bread?*
> B: *It takes several hours (to make bread).*

These sentences describe the time that is necessary to do something.

Practice

A Write *there is*, *there are*, *it is*, or *they are*.

▶ <u>There are</u> .... two ice rinks in our town; <u>they are</u> both near my house.

1 .... one train on Sundays; .... an express train.

2 .... two statutory holidays this month, and .... both on Fridays.

3 .... several trees in our yard, but .... not very tall.

4 .... a big lake in the park; .... very deep.

B Write answers to the questions using *there were … of* and the words in parentheses ( ).

▶ A: How many people were there at your party?
  B: (twenty/us) <u>There were twenty of us.</u>

1 A: How many of you were there in the car?
  B: (five/us) ....

2 A: How many Mounties were there in the building?
  B: (six/them) ....

3 A: How many people were there at the dinner party?
  B: (twelve/us) ....

C Rewrite the sentences using the words in parentheses ( ) and *it* or *there*.

▶ There's a lot of snow in December.
(snows a lot) _It snows a lot in December._

▶ It's very windy this morning.
(a lot of wind) _There's a lot of wind this morning._

1 There's a lot of rain in April.
(rains a lot) ....

2 It's icy on the highway this morning.
(ice on the highway) ....

3 There are a lot of clouds in the mountains.
(very cloudy) ....

4 It's very windy on the east coast.
(a lot of wind) ....

D Use *there* and the words in the box to complete the sentences. Use each word in the box once.

have been	~~is~~	may be	used to be	was	will be

▶ _There is_ .... an accident on this road almost every day.

1 Last year .... a terrible fire at that factory.

2 Next Monday at 7 p.m. .... a meeting of the committee.

3 When I was young, ... a lot more theatres than there are now.

4 Since 1900 .... two world wars.

5 .... a late-night bus, but I'm not sure if there is.

E Look at the times needed to prepare certain foods, then write a statement or a question and answer.

bake bread	– about three hours
~~make a salad~~	– ~~about ten minutes~~
make pancakes	– about twenty minutes
cook an omelette	– a few minutes
~~boil an egg~~	– ~~about three minutes~~
make coffee	– about five minutes.
make a cake	– about an hour.

▶ It _takes about three minutes to boil_ ....an egg.

▶ A: How long _does it take to make a salad_ .... ?
B: _It takes about ten minutes_ ....

1 It .... an omelette.

2 A: How long .... coffee?
B: ....

3 It .... bread.

4 A: How long .... pancakes?
B: ....

5 It .... cake.

So and such

We use **so** and **such** to intensify adjectives. Compare:

1 *Helen got all the answers right. She is **so** smart.* (= She is very smart.)

*Helen got all the answers right. She is **such a** smart person.* (= She is a very smart person.)

We use **so** before adjectives that do not have a noun after them, and before adverbs:

	ADJECTIVE
*This pop is **so***	*sweet!*
*Tom's feet are **so***	*big!*

	ADVERB
*They get up **so***	*late.*
*Maria sang **so***	*beautifully!*

We use **such a/an** before an adjective + singular noun (e.g. **person**). We use **such** before a plural noun (e.g. **feet**) or an uncountable noun (e.g. **food**):

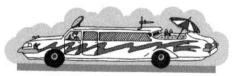

	ADJECTIVE + NOUN
*It was **such an***	*amazing car!*
*He has **such***	*big feet!*
*That was **such***	*excellent food.*

2 We can use **so** with **many** and **much**:

▶ **so many** + plural noun:
*There were **so many** people at the rodeo.*

▶ **so much** + uncountable noun:
*We had **so much** work to do.*

We can use **such** with **a lot of**:

▶ **such a lot of** + plural noun:
*There were **such a lot of people** at the rodeo.*

▶ **such a lot of** + uncountable noun:
*We had **such a lot of work** to do.*

3 Sentences with **so** and **such** can also describe the result of something:

	RESULT
*It was **so** dark*	*that we didn't see him.*
*He arrived **so** late,*	*he missed his plane.*

	RESULT
*It was **such a** dark night*	*that we didn't see him.*
*It was **such a** lovely day,*	*we went to the beach.*

Practice

A **Complete each sentence with *such* or *so*.**

▶ Omar is very handsome. He has ~~such~~ beautiful eyes.
▶ It was a very pleasant trip because the guide was ~~so~~ nice.
1 My birthday was wonderful. I got .... wonderful presents.
2 It was difficult to drive because there was .... much snow.
3 I like Riyaad. He is .... a nice person.
4 We couldn't play tennis because it was .... windy.
5 Jack loves his children. He is .... a wonderful father.
6 Nobody listens to Jane because she says .... silly things.
7 The nurses are wonderful here. They are .... helpful.
8 Look at the stars. They are .... bright tonight.

B Write *such*, *such a*, or *such an* in the blanks.

▶ Halifax is _such a_ wonderful city.
1 Motorcycles are .... dangerous machines.
2 I love skiing. It's .... exciting sport. But it's a dangerous sport, too.
3 My cousin had .... terrible accident. He almost died.
4 I like these new dresses. They have .... pretty colours.
5 We had .... wonderful meal. The food was excellent.
6 Margaret Atwood is .... interesting writer.

C Use *so*, *such*, *such a*, or *such an* to write sentences using the words in parentheses ( ).
Put the verbs in the correct tense.

▶ I can't believe that Dino is only thirteen. (He/have/grow/tall)
He has grown so tall!

▶ I never believe those boys. (They/be/always/tell/stupid lies)
They are always telling such stupid lies!

1 I enjoy John's cooking. (He/be/wonderful cook)
....

2 I can't hear anything. (Those people/be/make/much noise)
....

3 Marc won three prizes. (He/be/lucky)
....

4 Sara always looks great. (She/wear/pretty clothes)
....

5 We had three ice cream cones. (They/be/delicious)
....

6 I don't smoke. (It/be/unhealthy habit)
....

7 I enjoyed that test. (It/be/easy)
....

D For each sentence, write another sentence with a similar meaning.
Use *so ... that*.

▶ We decided not to call them because it was very late.
It was _so late that we decided not to call them._
1 Veronique didn't finish the exam because she worked very slowly.
She worked ....
2 We didn't buy the camera because it was very expensive.
The camera was ....
3 Paul didn't go out because he was very tired.
Paul was ....
4 Oscar couldn't see the holes because they were very small.
The holes were ....
5 I couldn't finish the food because there was too much of it.
There was ....

Adjective + preposition

1 Some adjectives can be followed by a **preposition + noun**:

ADJECTIVE	+ PREPOSITION	+ NOUN
I'm afraid	*of*	*dogs.*
She's good	*at*	*math.*

Here are some more examples:
afraid of: *I'm afraid of storms.*
angry at/with: *John is very angry with me.*
annoyed with: *I was annoyed with my sister.*
busy with: *Tom was busy with his work.*
careless with: *Bill is careless with his money.*
cruel to: *Ann's mother was cruel to her.*
famous for: *France is famous for its cheese.*
fond of: *Peter is very fond of reading.*
frightened of: *Our cat is frightened of your dog.*
full of: *The rooms were full of old furniture.*
good at: *Are you good at lacrosse?*
grateful for: *They were grateful for our help.*
interested in: *She's interested in old coins.*
kind to: *Your sister was very kind to us.*
lucky at: *I'm often lucky at games.*
pleased with: *Ian was pleased with the result.*
proud of: *They're proud of their children.*
sure about: *Are you sure about her name?*
surprised by: *I was surprised by her anger.*

2 Some adjectives are followed by a **preposition + -ing form**:

ADJECTIVE	+ PREPOSITION + -ing FORM	
He was	*sick of washing*	*dishes.*

*I'm not very **good at running**.*
*Robert is very **fond of talking**.*
*Natalia is **used to working** at night.*
  (= She often works at night, and she doesn't mind it.)

3 A few adjectives can have an **-ing** form without a preposition:

busy	no good	not worth

ADJECTIVE + -ing FORM	
busy getting	

They were **busy getting** *things ready.*

*It's **no good worrying** about the weather.*
*It's **not worth taking** the car, we can walk.*

Practice

A **Write the missing prepositions (e.g. with, of).**

▶ Alyssa was pleased _with_ her exam results. She got good marks in most subjects.
1 Thank you very much. I am very grateful .... your help.
2 I'm not sure .... the price, but I think they cost about $5.
3 It was the day of the concert, and everyone was busy .... the preparations.
4 I didn't expect to win the game. I was surprised .... the result.
5 Sandra was very brave. We are very proud .... her.
6 I like geography and I'm very interested .... history as well.
7 We've got plenty of food. The fridge is full .... things to eat.
8 Jenna didn't like the director. She was annoyed .... him.
9 John is very smart. He's good .... physics and chemistry.
10 Jane doesn't like small animals, but she's very fond .... horses.
11 Jeff should look after his laptop. He's very careless .... it.

12 Terry and Beverley like sports. They are particularly interested .... hockey.

13 Colin must be good .... French. He got a great mark on his test.

14 Mike has never learned to swim because he's afraid .... the water.

B Write these short dialogues in the Simple Present. Use the words in parentheses ( ) and any prepositions (e.g. *with*, *of*, *at*) that you need.

▶ A: (Julie, why/be/you/angry/Jeremy?)   ~ B: (Because he/be/very careless/his money)

A: *Julie, why are you angry with Jeremy?*

B: *Because he is very careless with his money.*

1 A: (be/their daughter/good/school work?)   ~ B: (Yes, in fact she/be/good/everything)

A: ....

B: ....

2 A: (Why/be/Mr. Lafleur's dog/afraid/him?)   ~ B: (Because he/be/often/cruel/it)

A: ....

B: ....

3 A: (be/Jenny/fond/classical music?)   ~ B: (Yes, she/be/very interested/
                                                                      Bach, for example)

A: ....

B: ....

4 A: (be/you/pleased/Peter's exam results?)   ~ B: (Yes, we/be/very proud/him)

A: ....

B: ....

C Complete the dialogue using the words in the box, and add a preposition if it is necessary.

busy	famous	full	good	interested	~~kind~~
no good	sick	used	worried	worth	

Terry: How did your job interview go?

Penny: All right, I think. The company director was very (▶) *kind to* .... me.

Terry: What does the company make?

Penny: Clothes. It's (1)........................ its athletic clothes, in fact. I had to wait for a while because the director was (2)........................ talking to some clients. The hallway where I waited was (3)........................ boxes with clothes in them.

Terry : And what did he ask you?

Penny: She. The director's a woman. She asked me if I was (4)........................ math. I said yes. She asked me if I was (5)........................ working under pressure, and I told her that I prefer to be busy at work so that it was no problem. Then she asked me why I was (6)........................ changing jobs, and I told her that I was (7)........................ working hard for so little pay. I'm a bit (8)........................ that answer now; perhaps it wasn't the best thing to say.

Terry : It's (9)........................ thinking about it now. What do you think your chances are?

Penny: I'm not sure. I'm not really sure that I want to change jobs just now, but I think it's (10)........................ going to an interview from time to time because it gives you practice and makes you more confident.

Position of adverbs in a sentence

1 There are a number of possible positions for adverbs:

- ▶ before the subject:
  Sometimes she gets very tired.
- ▶ between the subject and the verb:
  I sometimes read biographies.
- ▶ between a modal or auxiliary and the main verb:
  I can sometimes play this game very well.
- ▶ at the end of a clause or sentence:
  He makes me angry sometimes.

However, not all adverbs can go in every position.

2 We use adverbs of certainty (**probably, certainly, definitely**) in these positions:

- ▶ between the subject and a positive verb:
  Jane probably knows the answer.
- ▶ after a positive auxiliary/modal:
  They'll probably win.
- ▶ before a negative auxiliary/modal:
  Jane probably doesn't know the answer.
  They probably won't win.

3 We use adverbs of completeness (**almost, nearly**, etc.) in these positions:

- ▶ between the subject and the verb:
  He almost died.
- ▶ after an auxiliary/modal:
  I am nearly finished.

4 We use some adverbs that emphasize a statement (**even, just** (= simply), **only, also**) in these positions:

- ▶ between the subject and the verb:
  She was rude and she even laughed at me.
  I don't know why, I just like jazz.
- ▶ after an auxiliary/modal:
  I can't even understand a word.
  I'm only joking.

Notice that we use **just** before a negative modal or auxiliary:
I just don't understand why it happened.

5 Note that all these adverbs go after **be**:
She is probably at work now.

6 We use **too** and **either** at the end of a sentence. We use **too** after two positive verbs and **either** after two negative verbs:
George earns a lot and he spends a lot, too.
I don't like dogs and I'm not a fan of cats, either.

7 We usually use adverbs of manner (those that describe how something is done, e.g. **well, badly, quickly, carefully**) in these positions:

- ▶ after the verb:
  Please drive carefully.
- ▶ after an object:
  I read the email carefully.

8 We use adverbial phrases of time (e.g. *in the morning, last Saturday, during our vacation*) at the beginning or end of a sentence or clause:
Last Saturday I had a great time.
I had a great time last Saturday.

We usually use other adverbial phrases (e.g. those describing place or manner) after the object:
He put his suitcase on the floor.
She opened the package with a knife.

9 When there is more than one adverb or adverbial phrase in a sentence, we normally use them in this order:

> manner → place → time

He was working hard in his office last night.

Practice

A Write sentences using the adverb in parentheses ( ) in the correct place.

- ▶ (probably) They will take the train. They will probably take the train.
- 1 (definitely) She is from Dog Creek. ....

2 (nearly) The meal is ready. ....
3 (even) He lent me some money. ....
4 (certainly) She works very hard. ....
5 (only) There were two tickets left. ....

B These sentences are taken from a newspaper's sports section but they are all incorrect. Rewrite them so that they are correct.

▶ He will play definitely in Saturday's game.
  <u>He will definitely play in Saturday's game.</u> ....

1 Tickets for the game almost have sold out.
  ....

2 They won't probably win the Stanley Cup.
  ....

3 He scored two goals and he got also two assists.
  ....

4 They didn't just play well enough to win.
  ....

5 They won nearly but they were unlucky at the end.
  ....

C These sentences are taken from movie reviews. Put the adverbs in parentheses ( ) into the correct position in the <u>underlined</u> parts of the sentences.

▶ This movie <u>will be</u> a big hit with audiences. (definitely)   <u>will definitely be</u> ....
1 Many of the characters and events <u>are unbelievable</u>. (almost)   ....
2 This movie <u>doesn't create</u> any interest or excitement. (just)   ....
3 The plot isn't very interesting and the performances <u>aren't</u>   ....
   <u>very good</u>. (either)
4 Although the movie <u>was released</u> last week, it has earned a lot   ....
   of money. (only)
5 This movie <u>has attracted</u> a lot of publicity. (certainly)   ....
6 She can act very well <u>and she can sing</u> very well. (also)   ....

D Put the words and phrases in the correct order to make sentences.

▶ hard/worked/yesterday
  Susan <u>worked hard yesterday.</u> ....
1 all day/have/well/worked
  They ....
2 after lunch/in the lake/swam
  The children ....
3 during the night/snowed/heavily
  It ....
4 before dinner/did/in my room/my homework
  I ....
5 better/last week/played
  Our team ....

Prepositions of place and movement

1 **In, on,** and **at** are used to talk about places:

> ▶ We use **in** with enclosed spaces (e.g. rooms, buildings) and limited areas (e.g. cities, provinces, countries, continents):
> *in my pocket   in her car   in Germany*

> ▶ We use **on** with surfaces (e.g. walls, floors, shelves) and lines (e.g. streets, coasts, the equator):
> *on the grass   on the west coast*
> *on Bay Street   on the third floor*

> ▶ We use **at** with a point (e.g. **at** the bus stop), and **at** with a building, when we mean either inside or outside:
> *A: Let's meet **at** the arena.*
> *B: OK. Shall we meet **in** the arena itself or **on** the sidewalk outside?*

2 Look at the illustration and read the sentences:

*There is a bank **in** the town.*
*There are people **outside** the theatre.*
*The people are **on** the sidewalk.*
*There is a clock **above** the theatre entrance.*
*The theatre entrance is **under** the clock.*
*The bank is **next to/beside** the theatre.*
*The bank is **between** the theatre and the café.*
*There is a hill **behind** the town.*
*The car is **in front of** the bank.*

3 **Into, onto,** and **to** are used to talk about movement:
> *We moved the chairs **into** my bedroom.*
> *The actor ran **onto** the stage.*
> *They walked **to** the next town.*

The opposites are **out of, off,** and **from:**
> *We moved the chairs **out of** my bedroom.*
> *The actor ran **off** the stage.*
> *We drove **from** Red Deer to Calgary.*

Here are other prepositions of movement:
> *They ran **across** the field to the road.*
> *Jim cycled **along** the road to the next town.*
> *I walked **up** the hill and ran **down** the other side.*
> *The bus went **past** the bus stop without stopping.*
> *The train goes **through** three tunnels.*

Practice

A The sentences below describe the picture. Look at the picture and change any incorrect underlined words. Check (✓) the underlined words which are correct.

> ▶ There is a TV <u>under</u> *on*............. the table.
> ▶ There is a dog <u>on</u> ✓............. the floor.
> 1 There is a picture <u>on</u> .... the wall.
> 2 The dog is <u>on</u> .... the table.
> 3 The TV is <u>in front of</u> .... the cat.
> 4 The bird is <u>in</u> .... a cage.
> 5 There are flowers <u>on</u> .... the flowerpot.
> 6 The table is <u>behind</u> .... the bird cage.
> 7 There is a book <u>above</u> .... the table.
> 8 The keys are <u>between</u> .... the cat and the flowers.

B Write *in*, *on*, or *at* in the blanks.

▶ Peter lives in...... Turkey.

1 I live .... Elgin Street .... Ottawa.
2 We stopped .... the intersection and waited for the traffic to stop.
3 Mathieu sat .... the car waiting for his mom to finish .... the bank.
4 She bought a house .... Main Street.
5 The dog slept .... the floor .... their bedroom.
6 I saw a football game .... Mosaic Stadium when I was .... Regina.

C Write the words from the box in the blanks.

| into (x2)   onto   to (x4)   out of (x2)   off (x2)   from |

1 My dog hates getting .... the car when he knows we're going ....
the vet. When we get .... the vet's office, he won't get .... the car.
He's much more cooperative when we're going .... the beach.

2 My two-year-old will get .... any cupboard that isn't locked. She will even drag
a chair .... the table .... the kitchen counter, then climb ....
the counter. Even though she has fallen .... the counter, she won't quit trying.
I can't keep her .... the counter and .... the cupboards.

D Look at this picture of a town showing the route for a race.

Now fill in the blanks using the words from the box.

| across   along   at   down   in front of   past   from   under   through   up |

The race starts (▶) at............. at the town hall. The runners go away (1)............... the
town hall and they run (2)............... the main square to the river. Then they run over New
Bridge and they go (3)............... the road beside the river for about 200 metres. They go
(4)............... the theatre and (5)............... Castle Hill. They turn right (6)...............
the castle, and they go (7)............... Steep Hill. Then they go (8)............... the tunnel
(9)............... the river, and they finish at the station.

Other uses of prepositions

There are many common phrases that have prepositions in them.

1 We use **at** in these phrases:

> **at the beginning/end of, at first, at last,**
> **at the moment, at six o'clock, at once**
> (= "immediately" or "at the same time")

> *She'll be back **at the beginning of** next week.*
> ***At first**, I didn't believe what he was saying.*
> *I waited for weeks and **at last** the letter*
> *arrived.*
> *Are you busy **at the moment**?*
> *You don't have to do everything **at once**.*

We also use **at** for speeds:
> *He was driving **at** over 150 km an hour.*

2 We use **by** with means of transportion:

> **by car/bike/bus/plane/boat/subway/train, etc.**

*Do you go to work **by subway** or **by car**?*
But we say **on foot** (= walking):
> *I came here **on foot** because I wanted to get*
> *some exercise.*

We use **in my, our,** etc./**the car** to talk about someone's car:
> *It was only a short trip but we went*
> *in **my/our/the car**.*

We use **on my, our,** etc. with **bike**:
> *He came **on his bike**.*

We use **on the** before other means of transportion:
> *They went to Montreal **on the train**.*

We use **by** in phrases describing processes (e.g. sending something, ordering something, paying for something, making something):
> *I'll send the information **by mail/email/fax**.*
> *Can you book tickets **by phone**?*
> *You can pay **by credit card** or **by cheque**.*
> *All these products were made **by hand**.*

But we say **in cash**:
> *I paid for the vacation **in cash**.*

We also use **by** in these phrases:
> **by chance, by accident, by mistake**

3 We use **for** in these phrases:

> **for example, for sale, forever**

> *Their house is **for sale**.*
> *I'd like to live here **forever**.*

4 We use **in** in these phrases:

> **in advance, in danger, in the future, in a**
> **hurry, in charge (of), in control, in fashion,**
> **in general, in love, in my opinion, in the past**

> *You should book a table **in advance**.*
> *I can't talk to you now, I'm **in a hurry**.*
> ***In general**, she has a good life.*

Notice also: **in writing/pen/pencil/capitals**
> *Please write your name **in capitals** in*
> *this box.*
> *Put your complaint **in writing**.*
> (= write a formal letter)

5 We use **on** in these phrases:

> **on business/on vacation/on a trip, on (the)**
> **TV/televison, on the radio, on the Internet,**
> **on (a/the) computer, on the phone**
> (= speaking, using it), **on strike, on fire, on**
> **the floor**

> *I'm going away **on vacation/on business***
> *next week.*
> *All this work is done **on computer** these days.*
> *There are no trains because the drivers are*
> ***on strike**.*
> *I found a lot of useful information **on the***
> ***internet**.*
> *She was **on the phone** when I went into*
> *the room.*

6 Notice also the common prepositions **except (for)** and **instead of**:
> *Everyone was happy **except (for)** Elaine.*
> (= Elaine was the only person who wasn't
> happy.)
> *I'd prefer a cold drink **instead of** coffee.*
We use an **-ing** form after **instead of**:
> *I walked to work **instead of going** by car.*

Practice

A Match the first and second parts of the sentences.

▶ I waited for ages until the package arrived at   a   fashion.
1 You should buy your tickets well in   b   strike.
2 As part of her job she has to travel a lot on   c   advance.
3 I didn't plan to meet him, it happened by   d   last.
4 I won't make the same mistake in   e   business.
5 There were no buses because the drivers were on   f   chance.
6 Those pants are currently in   g   the future.

▶ d...... 1 .... 2 .... 3 .... 4 .... 5 .... 6 ....

B Complete these official instructions by writing the correct prepositions.

▶ We can be contacted by............. phone at the number below.
1 Complaints must be put .... writing and sent to the address below.
2 Please complete your personal details .... capitals.
3 Applications sent .... mail will be dealt with as soon as possible.
4 Payment can be made .... credit card or .... cheque but not .... cash.
5 Feel free to contact me .... email at any time.

C Complete this email to a friend by using these words and the correct prepositions in the blanks.

| first | vacation | once | ~~hurry~~ | charge | ever | example | mistake |

Hi Pete,
I've been living in this city for a couple of months now. It's a very crowded and
busy place and everyone seems to be (▶) in a hurry............ all the time. Nobody is willing
to wait for anything, they want to have it (1)......................... . I see this all the time.
(2)........................ , I was in a restaurant the other day and the man at the next table
demanded to speak to the person (3)........................ because he'd been waiting five
minutes for his meal! When the waiter then brought the wrong meal (4)........................ ,
he went blew up! (5)........................ I thought I'd like living here, but now I've decided it's
a good place to visit (6)........................ . I wouldn't want to live here (7)........................ ·
Rick

D Complete these sentences with the correct prepositions.

▶ Did you have a good time on............. the weekend?
1 .... my opinion, you're wasting your time.
2 A few minutes later, the whole building was .... fire.
3 They've been .... love ever since they first met.
4 They've won every game .... one, which they lost badly.
5 She does most of her work .... a computer.

Relative clauses (1)

1 In informal English, in defining relative clauses, when **who, that,** or **which** is the object of the verb, it can be omitted:

> *The name of the woman I interviewed was Mrs. Norris.*
> *The car they bought was very expensive.*

Notice that there is no pronoun in the relative clause:

> *The name of the woman I interviewed ~~her~~ was Mrs. Norris.*
> *The car they bought ~~it~~ was very expensive.*

2 When the verb has a preposition, in formal English the preposition goes with **whom** or **which**:

> *That is the young man **to whom** I spoke.*
> *The job **for which** she's applied is in Lethbridge.*

Informally, we can omit the relative word and then the preposition goes at the end of the relative clause:

> *That is the young man I spoke **to**.*
> *The job she's applied **for** is in Lethbridge.*

3 Informally, we often omit the relative word **when** after **day, year,** etc.:

> *That was the **year** I finished university.*

We often omit the relative word **where** after **place, somewhere,** etc.:

> *Do you know **a place / somewhere** we can get a good sandwich?*

We often omit the relative word **why** after **reason:**

> *The real **reason** she came was to speak to my father.*

We often omit a relative expression after **way:**

> *That's the **way** they greet each other in Quebec.*

Practice

A In the following sentences, cross out the words that are not possible or not necessary. If there are no such words, mark the sentence with a check (✓).

▶ The first book ~~which~~ he wrote ~~it~~ was *Subconscious Selling*. ....

▶ This is the boy who broke the window. ✓......

1 Do you know the woman that my father's talking to? ....

2 They're going to close the factories that they make too much smog. ....

3 People who live in small apartments shouldn't have dogs. ....

4 An animal that comes out at night must have good eyes. ....

5 The canoe that my cousins paddled in it was overturned by a wave. ....

6 An amphibian is an animal which can live on land or in water. ....

7 People who are from Labrador are called Labradorians. ....

B In the following, if a sentence is incomplete, indicate where a word is necessary and write the word at the end. If the sentence is correct, mark it with a check (✓).

▶ Is there a store near here sells stamps?
   Is there a store near here╱sells stamps? <u>that</u>..............

▶ Mrs. Thomas is the teacher my sister likes best. ✓......................

1 The referee is the person makes the decisions. ....

2 The bus they were waiting for never came. ....

3 The elderly lady we saw was wearing a pink dress. ....

4 Is this the train goes to Edmonton? ....

5 There's a place near here you can get a good hamburger. ....

6 It took a long time to find the doctor we wanted to see. ....

7 Do you know anybody plays the piano really well? ....

C In each case, combine the two sentences into one. Write *who*, *that*, *which*, or *where* only if it is necessary.

▶ I lent you a book. Have you read it?

   Have you read the book I lent you ....?

▶ My mother works in a factory. It makes parts for cars.

   The factory where my mother works .... makes parts for cars.

1 Sharon's got a new cellphone. It takes great photos.

   Sharon's got a new cellphone ....

2 They lived in an apartment building. It was struck by lightning.

   The apartment building .... was struck by lightning.

3 The hotel had a bartender. He made very good Caesars.

   The hotel had a bartender ....

4 The miners are paid a salary. They can't live on it.

   The miners can't live on the salary ....

5 Nobody else wanted the food. My father ate it.

   My father ate the food ....

6 We ran out of gas in a small town. It didn't have a gas station.

   The town .... didn't have a gas station.

D Freda and Len are packing to go on vacation. Complete the conversation with the expressions from the box and include *that* if it is necessary.

you can take as a carry-on	go with my green dress	has a lock
have just been re-soled	I knitted myself	needs film
we can walk all day in	covers all the Mediterranean islands	
we bought in that used bookstore		

Len: We'd better take two suitcases. The one (▶) that has a lock ....
      and that smaller one (1) ....

Freda: Which camera do you want to take? The digital one or the old one
      (2) .... ?

Len: Let's take the digital one. How about the travel guide? There's that big one
      (3) .... and that smaller one – the one just
      about Corsica (4) ....

Freda: Perhaps the small one will be enough.

Len: I think I'll take my shoes (5) .... How many
      pairs of shoes are you taking?

Freda: Well, we'll need some comfortable ones (6) ....
      and perhaps for the evenings I'll take the new green ones, the ones
      (7) ....

Len: It might be cool in the evenings. I suppose you're taking a sweater.

Freda: Yes, the white one. You know, the one (8) ....
      Anyway, let's take a break. I feel like a drink.

Relative clauses (2)

1 Look at these two sentences:

Ottawa has almost 1 million inhabitants.
*Ottawa, **which is the capital of Canada,** has almost 1 million inhabitants.*

The clause **which is the capital of Canada** gives us more information about Ottawa, but we do not need this information to define **Ottawa**. We can understand the first sentence without this extra information. **which is the capital of Canada** is a non-defining relative clause. It has commas (,) to separate it from the rest of the sentence.

2 For things or animals, we use **which** (BUT NOT ~~that~~) in non-defining relative clauses:
   *Kim sold his computer, **which he no longer needed,** to his cousin. (NOT … ~~that he no longer needed~~ …)*
   *In the summer we stay in my uncle's house, **which is in the Rockies.***

3 For people, we use **who** (but not **that**) in non-defining relative clauses. We use **who** when it is the subject of the relative clause:

Elvis Presley, | SUBJECT |
| who | died in |
1977, earned millions of dollars.
(**Presley** died in 1977.)

We use **who** (or sometimes **whom**) when it is the object of the relative clause:

| OBJECT |
My boss, | who (or whom) | *I last saw before Christmas, is very sick.*
(I last saw **my boss** before Christmas.)

4 We use **whose** to mean "his," "her," or "their":
   *Marilyn Monroe, **whose real name was Norma Jean,** was born in Los Angeles.*
   (**Her** real name was Norma Jean.)

5 We can also use **which** (BUT NOT ~~that~~) to refer to a whole fact:
   | *Ann did not want to marry Tom* |*, which surprised everybody.*

Here, **which** refers to the fact that Ann did not want to marry Tom.

Practice

A Make one sentence from the two that are given. Use *who* or *which*.

▶ Mont Blanc is between France and Italy. It is the highest mountain in the Alps.
   Mont Blanc, which is between France and Italy, is the highest mountain in the Alps.

▶ Atom Egoyan was born in Egypt. He made many successful films.
   Atom Egoyan, who was born in Egypt, made many successful films.

1 The sun is really a star. It is 150 million kilometres from the earth.

   ....

2 Pierre Trudeau died in 2000. He was a very famous prime minister.

   ....

3 Charlie Chaplin was from a poor family. He became a very rich man.

   ....

4 The 2010 Olympics were held in Vancouver. It is on the west coast.

   ....

5 We went to see the Big Nickel. It is in Sudbury.

   ....

B From the notes, write one sentence. Use *who*, *whose*, or *which* with the words in parentheses ( ).

▶ Greta Garbo. (She was born in Sweden.) She moved to the US in 1925.
  Greta Garbo, who was born in Sweden, moved to the US in 1925.

▶ Darwin. (His ideas changed our view of the world.) He travelled a lot when he was young.
  Darwin, whose ideas changed our view of the world, travelled a lot when he was young.

1 Soccer. (It first started in Britain.) It is now popular in many countries.
  Soccer, ...

2 Brian Mulroney. (He was the prime minister of Canada for nine years.) He studied political science in university.
  ....

3 Michelangelo. (He lived until he was 90.) He was one of Italy's greatest artists.
  ....

4 Bill Clinton. (His wife became the Secretary of State.) He was elected President of the US in 1992.
  ....

5 The Nile. (It runs through several countries.) It is the longest river in Africa.
  ....

6 Madonna. (Her parents were born in Italy.) She is a popular singer.
  ....

7 Gandhi. (He was born in 1869). He was assassinated in 1948.
  ....

8 Elephants. (They are found in Africa and India). They are sometimes hunted for their ivory.
  ....

9 The Beatles. (Their music is still popular.) They were probably the most famous pop group in the world.
  ....

10 Calgary. (It is in Alberta.) It is famous for its annual rodeo.
  ....

C Complete this paragraph about Lewis Carroll by writing *who*, *which*, or *whose* in the blanks.

Alice in Wonderland, (▶) which......... is one of the most popular children's books in the world, was written by Lewis Carroll, (1)............... real name was Charles Dodgson. Carroll, (2)............... had a natural talent as a story-teller, loved to entertain children, including Alice Liddell, (3)............... father was a colleague of Carroll's at Oxford University. One day Carroll took Alice and her sisters for a trip on the River Thames, (4)............... flows through Oxford. After the trip, Carroll wrote in his diary that he had told the children a wonderful story, (5)............... he had promised to write down for them. He wrote the story, illustrated it with his own drawings, and gave it to the children. By chance, it was seen by Henry Kingsley, (6)............... was a famous novelist, and he persuaded Dodgson to publish it.

Since, as, for

1 We can use **because**, **since**, and **as** to express a reason for something. Normally we use **because** when the reason has not been mentioned previously; the reason usually comes in second place:

> We stayed at home *because Darcy was sick.*

If the conversation has already mentioned that Darcy was sick, we normally express the reason with **since** or **as**; the reason usually comes in first place:

> Darcy wasn't feeling well. *Since / As Darcy was sick, we stayed at home.*

2 We can use **for** to express purpose or reason with different structures. We can use it with a noun to express a purpose:

> I went to the store *for some cheese.*
> We stopped *for a drink.*

3 When the action and the purpose involve different people, we express this with **for** and a noun or pronoun followed by the infinitive with **to**:

> We stopped *for the children to have a drink.*
> I waited *for him to finish his homework.*

4 We can use **for** with a noun or an **-ing** form to give the reason for a reaction:

> The teacher sent Jill home *for cheating.*
> My cousin was arrested *for robbery.*

Johnson is in prison *for dangerous driving.*
Sam won a medal *for saving a young boy.*

Here the reason happens before the reaction.

5 You will sometimes see **for** used in a way similar to **because**:

> Diane was happy to receive the books, *for she loved reading.*

However, this is not common and you can always use **because** in these cases.

6 We can also use the preposition **due to** (and, less often, **owing to**) with a noun to express a reason:

> Many people arrived late *due to / owing to the heavy rain.*
> *Due to / Owing to* the road repairs, we had to take a different route.

If we use these prepositions with a clause, we have to include **the fact that**:

> The concert was cancelled *due to/owing to the fact that* the pianist had appendicitis.

Note that we can use **noun + be + due to + noun**:

> The delay *was due to heavy snow.*

We cannot use **owing to** in this way:

> NOT ~~The delay was owing to heavy snow.~~

Here the reason happens before the action or fact.

Practice

A Complete the sentences with an expression from the box.

due to a problem with the brakes	~~for a cup of coffee~~	for some ketchup
for the best drawing	for the children	owing to the transit strike
since Carolyn's a vegetarian		

▶ The men took a break *for a cup of coffee* .

1 She kept a box of toys .... to play with.

2 Sandra won a prize ....

3 .... , we can't take her to our usual restaurant.

4 Jane's accident was ....

5 Jack has gone to the store ....

6 Many people were late for work ....

B In each question, complete the second sentence so that it means the same as the first. In some cases, there is more than one possibility.

▶ Sue went to the kitchen to get some ice cubes.
Sue went to the kitchen for *some ice cubes* ....

1 Mother sent Timmy to bed because he insulted her.
Mother sent Timmy to bed for ....

2 The ferry was late due to the heavy winds.
The ferry was late due to .... it was very windy.

3 Ken hit his sister and his father punished him.
Ken's father punished him for ....

4 We had the meeting in the annex because they were repairing the main building.
We had the meeting in the annex owing to .... the main building.

5 The boss gave Terry a bonus because he worked on the weekend.
The boss gave Terry a bonus for .... on the weekend.

6 I can't get into the bathroom because Debbie's in there.
Since ...., I can't get in there.

7 The road is blocked because some trees have fallen.
The blocked road is due to ....

8 They waited while the moose crossed the road.
They waited for .... cross the road.

C Here is a story about a day out for the Ling family. Complete the story by choosing the correct option in each case.

Mr. Ling is a careless driver. In fact he has a reputation as a dangerous driver (▶) because/~~owing to~~ the police have fined him three times (1) because/for speeding. (2) Due to/Since he drives carelessly, his wife usually drives the family car, especially when the children are with them. The children often feel sick in the car (3) due to the fact that/owing to they are not good travellers, and when this happens Mrs. Ling has to stop the car (4) for/as them to take a break. Some people take pills for travel sickness, of course, but Mrs. Ling doesn't like the idea (5) because/due to she thinks the children will get addicted. One hot summer's day, the family was on the way to visit Mrs. Ling's mother (6) owing to the fact that/owing to it was her birthday. (7) Since/For it was a special day the children were wearing their nicest clothes, so it was obviously a bad day (8) for/because them to get dirty. Very soon the children were feeling sick, probably due (9) to/for the heat, so Mrs. Ling stopped the car several times (10) for/since them to get out and have a drink. When they finally arrived, Grandma said, "You're a bit late but I suppose that's (11) due to/owing to the traffic." "Not really," said Mrs. Ling. "The trip took longer than usual (12) because/owing to the heat and the fact that we had to stop several times (13) to/for a break." At their grandmother's, the children soon felt better and they had a great afternoon. After lunch they went for long walk with Grandma's dog, Fluffy. On the way home they were tired and fell asleep in the car.

Although, while, however, despite, etc.

1 We can contrast two ideas or situations within a sentence with **although**:
> *Although the weather was very cold, we decided to go for a walk.*
> *The government passed the new law **although** many people opposed it.*

Informally we can use **though** in the same way:
> *Though the weather was very cold, we decided to go for a walk.*
> *The government passed the new law **though** many people opposed it.*

While is not possible here.

2 We can use **while** to contrast two aspects of the same thing or two similar things within a sentence:
> *While I agree with the idea, I don't think it's very practical.*
> *Some of my friends have found work **while** others are still unemployed.*

(Al)though is also possible here.

3 When the contrast is expressed in a separate sentence, we use **however**:
> *The government passed the new law.*
> *However, many people were against it.*

> *I agree with the idea. I don't think it's very practical, **however**.*

We use a comma to separate **however** from the rest of the sentence.

Though can also go at the end of a separate sentence:
> *I agree with the idea. I don't think it's very practical, **though**.*

Although is not possible here.

4 We can use prepositions **in spite of** and **despite** with a noun (but not usually a personal pronoun) to express concession or contrast:
> *In spite of / Despite the cold weather, we decided to go for a walk.*
> *The government passed the new law **in spite of / despite** the opposition.*

If we use these prepositions with a clause, we have to include **the fact that**, e.g.:
> *The government passed the new law **in spite of / despite the fact that** many people were against it.*

Practice

A **In each question, complete the second sentence (or pair of sentences) so that the meaning is the same as the first sentence (or pair of sentences).**

▶ Larry is older than Meg but she is taller than he is.
  Although Larry is older than Meg, she is taller than he is .

1 In spite of the fact that it was dangerous, many people helped in the rescue.
  Many people helped in the rescue although ....

2 Many people continue to smoke cigarettes although there is a serious warning on every package.
  .... the warning on every package, many people continue to smoke cigarettes.

3 There were several more experienced teams but the Oilers won the Cup.
  There were several more experienced teams. The Oilers won the Cup, ...

4 Although Toronto is more expensive than the rest of Ontario, many people prefer to live there.
  Many people prefer to live in Toronto despite ....
  it is more expensive than the rest of Ontario.

5 My job is interesting but it does not pay very well.
   While .... , it does not pay very well.
6 Although Amy complained about the exam, she got a very good mark.
   Amy complained about the exam. .... , she got
   a very good mark.

B Complete this speech about drugs by putting in *although*, *despite*, *however*, or *while*.
   In some cases there is more than one possibility.

Ladies and gentlemen. Today I want to explain why I think drugs should be legalized. Many
people think that all drugs are illegal. (▶) However.............. , the legal situation is different in
different countries. For example, (1)........................ coca leaves are legal in some parts of
South America, they are banned in Canada and many other countries. But even in Canada
and the US, it is not true that all drugs are illegal. (2)........................ tobacco and alcohol
are seriously addictive, they are a regular aspect of most social gatherings in our countries. Not
everybody who smokes tobacco or drinks alcohol is an addict, of course. Many regular smokers
would like to cut down or stop, (3)........................ , and in fact many have tried several times.
(4)........................ their many attempts, they continue smoking, precisely because nicotine
is so addictive. Anyway, what are the disadvantages of the illegal drugs remaining illegal? In the
first place, illegality means that there is no quality control to protect the consumer. People think
they are buying cocaine, for example, (5)........................ the substance is perhaps mixed
with dust or even poisonous powders. Also, drugs on the street are fairly expensive so
(6)........................ consumers might not have a job, they need their drugs and this quickly
leads to stealing and prostitution in order to pay for them. Second, the drug industry generates
enormous quantities of money, enough money to corrupt many police officers and politicians.
We like to think that our authorities control crime. The reality, (7)........................ , is that in
some countries crime controls the authorities. Ladies and gentleman, (8)........................
you may not like drugs, as long as drugs are illegal, they are outside the government's control.

C Later, two people discuss the talk about drugs. Use each expression from the box
   once to complete the dialogue.

~~although~~	although	despite	however	in spite of the fact that	though

Tony: What did you think of the talk?
Pam: I don't agree with her (▶) although............. I have to accept that her talk was
       interesting. It's true that the present situation isn't perfect. (1)........................ ,
       if they legalize drugs, things will be much worse.
Tony: Oh, I don't know. Society seems to manage all right with tobacco and alcohol
       (2)........................ they're perfectly legal.
Pam: You make it sound as if they're harmless. I think it's more accurate to say that
       society functions (3)........................ they're legal because they cause problems
       for a lot of people.
Tony: A few people misuse them. Most people use them sensibly, (4)........................ .
Pam: It doesn't make sense to say that you can smoke sensibly. That's why there
       are health warnings on the packages. People are stupid enough to smoke
       (5)........................ all the warnings.

Because, in case, so, so that

1 We use **because** to give the reason for something:

Mohammad is in bed | **because** he's got the flu. — REASON

We couldn't go out **because** the weather was terrible.

I took a taxi **because** I was in a hurry.

We use **because of** with a noun (e.g. **flu, weather, noise**):

Mohammad's in bed | **because of** his flu. — REASON

We couldn't go out **because of** the storm.

I couldn't sleep **because of** the noise.

2 We use **in case** when the reason is something that might happen:

I'm taking an umbrella | **in case** it rains. — REASON

(= I'm taking an umbrella because it might rain.)

I'll call Patrick now, **in case** he wants to go with us.

(= ... because he might want to go with us.)

3 We use **so** to talk about the result of something:

I was in a hurry | **so** I took a taxi. — RESULT

Mohammad has the flu **so** he's in bed.

The weather was terrible **so** we couldn't go out.

My neighbours were having a party and making a lot of noise **so** I couldn't sleep.

4 We use **so that** to talk about the purpose of an action:

I took a taxi | **so that** I would arrive on time. — PURPOSE

I listen to the news in the morning **so that** I know what's happening in the world.

Tom goes jogging every day **so that** he'll stay in shape.

I took a taxi **so that** my friends would not have to wait for me.

(We can also use **to + infinitive** to talk about purpose; see page 54.)

Practice

A Write each sentence in a different way using the words given.

▶ Edwin didn't want to go out because he had a cold.
Edwin didn't want to go out .... because of _his cold_ ....

▶ Take some money because you might need to take a taxi.
Take some money .... in case _you need to take a taxi_ ....

▶ John and I asked for a drink because we were thirsty.
John and I were thirsty .... so _we asked for a drink_ ....

1 Vanessa went to bed because she was tired.
.... so ....

2 I couldn't sleep because it was so hot.
.... the heat.

3 Jill doesn't like apples so she doesn't eat them.
.... because ....

4 The streets were crowded because of the festival.
.... there was a festival.

5 I'll give Jane a key to the house because she might get home before me.
.... in case ....

B Complete the sentences with *because*, *in case*, or *so*, and a phrase from the box. Use each phrase once.

I'll take a book to read	his passport was expired
I want to lose weight	his wife was sick
she's at home	there is another power outage this weekend
~~they had to wait for the next one~~	

▶ They missed one bus *so they had to wait for the next one.*

1 I don't know where my sister is, but I'll try calling her ....

2 I'm eating healthier food these days ....

3 Peter had trouble at the airport ....

4 It's a long trip ....

5 We bought some candles ....

6 Mr. Ruiz didn't go to the meeting ....

C Write complete sentences using the words in parentheses ( ), making any necessary changes and including *so that*.

▶ (Sean/go/swimming every day/he can stay healthy.)
Sean goes swimming every day so that he can stay healthy. ....

1 (Last week, my brother/lend/me $40/I could buy some new shoes.)
....

2 (Last month, the government/pass/new traffic laws/fewer people will have accidents.)
....

3 (Our school has/open/a new library/we can have more books.)
....

4 (Ann always/write/everything in her agenda/she doesn't forget her appointments.)
....

5 (Last Friday, we/leave/home early/we could avoid the morning traffic.)
....

D If the sentence is correct, put a check (✓). If it is incorrect, cross out any incorrect words and, if necessary, write in the correct word.

▶ A: Why are they tired? ✓.............
  B: Because ~~that~~ their long trip. *of*.............

1 I can't work tomorrow, so that I worked today. ....

2 Take a sandwich with you in case you get hungry. ....

3 Julie had to go to the grocery store so she needed something for lunch. ....

4 A: Why are you here? ....
  B: I'm here for bring my son for his dental check-up. ....
  A: Well, since you're here, so we can check your teeth as well. ....

Review test

Choose the correct answer (a, b, c, d) and write a, b, c, or d, as in the example.
The correct answers are on page 105.

Russia is the .....*a*..... country in the world.
a largest   b larger   c most large   d most largest

Verbs and tenses

1 Where .... Tracy work?
  a does   b do   c are   d is

2 What .... , Hong?
  a you are   b are you   c do you   d are you doing

3 It's very cold today and ....
  a it's snowing   b it snows   c its snowing   d it snowing

4 They .... last week.
  a didn't come   b came not   c don't came   d didn't came

5 I didn't hear the phone because when it rang, I .... a shower.
  a took   b was taking   c had taken   d taking

6 When Carol was younger, she .... in a folk band.
  a use to sing   b sang usually   c was singing   d used to sing

7 Have you .... to Sri Lanka?
  a ever been   b ever gone   c been ever   d gone ever

8 My husband and I .... to Charlottetown in 2010.
  a have moved   b moved   c did moved   d has moved

9 I .... to Victoria five times already this week.
  a went   b have gone   c have been   d was going

10 I'm a vegetarian. I .... meat since I was a child.
  a haven't eaten   b don't eat   c haven't been eating   d am not eating

11 When we arrived, the train .... the station.
  a already left   b had already left   c had left already   d has left already

12 My cousins .... visit us next weekend.
  a will to   b going to   c are going to   d are going

13 Can somebody come and help me? ~ Yes, ... you.
  a I'll help   b I'm helping   c I will to help   d I help

14 If I .... you, I'd go to the police.
    a would be   b should be   c were   d am

15 I wish I .... to bed earlier last night.
    a went   b had gone   c was going   d have gone

16 We're going to .... some shopping.
    a make   b get   c do   d have

17 The plane .... in bad weather.
    a pulled off   b put up   c got up   d took off

18 There was no truth to his story. He simply ....
    a made up it   b made it up   c drew it out   d drew out it

Modal and other verbs

19 Who's the woman in that car? ~ .... be Luisa. She's in Germany.
    a It must not   b She must not   c It can't   d She can't

20 It's a present, so you .... pay anything.
    a don't get to   b haven't to   c must not to   d don't have to

21 We've got enough blue paint. Your sister .... to buy any more.
    a don't need   b doesn't need   c needs   d hasn't need

22 If you have stomach pains, you .... to go to the doctor.
    a had better   b should   c ought   d must

23 .... wear a uniform when you were in school?
    a Must you have worn   b Must you wear
    c Had you to wear   d Did you have to

Passive

24 Fiat .... a group of Italian businessmen.
    a is started for b is started by   c was started by   d was started for

25 Oh, no! My camera isn't here. It .... stolen!
    a has been   b is   c is being   d has

26 His hair is too long. He should .... cut.
    a let it be   b get it be   c make it   d have it

Infinitives and -ing forms

27 Would you .... to the theatre?
    a to like go   b like to go   c like going   d to like to going

28 I'm going to India next year. .... Kerala, Goa, and Mumbai.
    a I'm going to plan visiting   b I plan visiting
    c I'm going to plan to visit   d I plan to visit

29 This is a machine .... boxes.
    a for make   b for to make   c for making   d to making

30 We invited .... come to the party.
    a them to   b to them   c that they   d that they

Reported speech

31 Your cousin .... she lived in a small apartment.
    a said me   b said to me   c told   d told me

32 Michelle had a lot of work and so she asked .... help her.
    a me to   b to me   c that I   d that I should

33 Do you know where .... ?
    a lives Joe   b do Joe lives   c does Joe live   d Joe lives

Articles

34 Are you a vegetarian? ~ Yes, I never eat ....
    a meat   b the meat   c some meat   d a meat

35 .... is my favourite art.
    a A music   b The music   c Music   d Some music

There and it

36 How many schools .... near here?
    a are they   b is there   c are there   d is it

Adjectives and adverbs

37 It was .... night that we didn't see the animals.
    a a so dark   b so a dark   c such a dark   d a such dark

38 The rooms were full .... old furniture.
    a of   b with   c from   d off

39 After 25 minutes, take the meat .... the oven.
    a out from   b out of   c from of   d from out

40 I think we can meet .... the bus stop.
    a on   b at   c in   d behind

41 The train has to go .... three tunnels.
    a across   b along   c through   d under

Prepositions

42 It was very late, but .... last we reached the hotel.
    a in the   b at the   c in   d at

43 He doesn't talk much and he doesn't listen much ....
    a too   b neither   c either   d as well

Building sentences

44 I received your letter dated March 22, ... I'm very grateful.
    a which   b that   c for which   d to which

45 Marc went to see the film *Avatar*, ... had already seen three times.
    a which   b which he   c that   d that he

46 His mother yelled at him ....
    a for laughing   b because laughing
    c for he laughed   d because of laughing

47 Most people go by train. The bus, ... , is cheaper and faster.
    a although   b despite   c while   d however

48 .... the fact that nobody thought he should do it, he did it.
    a However   b While   c In spite of   d Because

49 Take your umbrella .... it rains.
    a because   b because of   c for   d in case

Appendix 1: Nouns

1 Plural nouns

1 We usually add -s to a noun to form the plural:

a book	→	some **books**
one kilogram	→	ten **kilograms**
radio	→	**radios**
loonie	→	**loonies**
canoe	→	**canoes**
tire	→	**tires**

2 After -s, -ss, -sh, -ch, and -x we add -es:

bus	→	**buses**	dress	→	**dresses**
glass	→	**glasses**	dish	→	**dishes**
wish	→	**wishes**	beach	→	**beaches**
watch	→	**watches**	box	→	**boxes**

3 When a noun ends in a consonant* + -y, the y changes to -ies:

city	→	**cities**	family	→	**families**
penny	→	**pennies**	story	→	**stories**

We do not change y after a vowel*:

day	→	**days**	alley	→	**alleys**

4 Nouns ending in -f or -fe have the plural -ves:

leaf	→	**leaves**	life	→	**lives**
shelf	→	**shelves**	thief	→	**thieves**

5 A few nouns ending in -o have -es:

potato	→	**potatoes**
tomato	→	**tomatoes**
hero	→	**heroes**

But most have -s:

photos	pianos	radios
stereos	studios	zoos

6 Some nouns have irregular plurals:

man	→	**men**	woman	→	**women**
child	→	**children**	foot	→	**feet**
mouse	→	**mice**	sheep	→	**sheep**
fish	→	**fish**	person	→	**people**
tooth	→	**teeth**	moose	→	**moose**

2 Uncountable nouns

1 Here is a list of common uncountable nouns:

ice	water	rain	snow
heat	noise	cotton	glass
gas	money	luggage	information
work	homework	advice	news
milk	butter	bread	cheese
tea	coffee	sugar	meat
jam	toast		

2 Uncountable nouns do not have a plural form:

heat (NOT ~~heats~~)   butter (NOT ~~butters~~)

3 We do not use ~~a/an~~ with uncountable nouns, but we can use **some/any**, **the**, **much** (NOT ~~many~~), **such** and **my/your/his**, etc.:

I always have **toast** and **jam** for breakfast.
I'd like **some coffee**, please.
Look at **the snow** outside.
How **much luggage** do you have?
We've had **such** wonderful **news**.

4 Some nouns can be countable or uncountable:

I heard a **noise** from downstairs.
(countable)
I can't sleep. The neighbours are making **so much noise**.
(uncountable)

---

* Consonants: b c d f g h j k l m n p q r s t v w x y z
Vowels: a e i o u
Syllables: |*hit*| = 1 syllable, |*vi*|*sit*| = 2 syllables,
|*re*|*mem*|*ber*| = 3 syllables

Appendix 2: Regular verbs

1 Simple Present

1 Add an -s to make the **he/she/it** form of most Simple Present verbs:

I/you/we/they	he/she/it
leave	*leaves*
make	*makes*
say	*says*
work	*works*

2 After -**ss**, -**sh**, -**ch**, -**o**, or -**x** (e.g. *finish, go*), we add -**es**:

I/you/we/they	he/she/it
catch	*catches*
finish	*finishes*
pass	*passes*
teach	*teaches*
do	*does*
go	*goes*
mix	*mixes*

3 When a verb ends in a consonant* + -**y**, the y changes to -**ies**:

I/you/we/they	he/she/it
fly	*flies*
try	*tries*
carry	*carries*
study	*studies*

2 The -ing form

1 For most verbs we add -**ing**:
   ask → *asking*   *go* → *going*

2 For verbs ending with a consonant + -**e**, we normally leave out **e** when we add -**ing**:
   hope → *hoping*   *live* → *living*
   take → *taking*
   But we keep a double **e** before -**ing**:
   see → *seeing*   *agree* → *agreeing*

3 When a verb ends in -**ie**, it changes to y when we add -**ing**:
   die → *dying*   *lie* → *lying*
   But **y** does not change:
   hurry → *hurrying*

4 When a word ends with one vowel* and one consonant (e.g. *run, swim, jog*), we double the final consonant:

   get → *getting*   *jog* → *jogging*
   run → *running*   *swim* → *swimming*
   But note that we do not double the consonant:
   • when it is **y**, **w**, or **x** (e.g. *stay*)
   buy → *buying*   *draw* → *drawing*
   wax → *waxing*   *stay* → *staying*
   • when the final syllable* is not stressed
   listen → *listening*   *visit* → *visiting*
   wonder → *wondering*
   Note, however, that in Canadian English **l** is usually doubled, even if the syllable is unstressed (e.g. *travel*):
   cancel → *cancelling*   *travel* → *travelling*

3 The past tense and past participles

1 Most verbs have -**ed** in the past tense; most past participles also end in -**ed**:

INFINITIVE	PAST TENSE	PAST/PASSIVE PARTICIPLE
happen	*happened*	*happened*
work	*worked*	*worked*

2 If the verb ends in -**e**, we add **d**:
   live → *lived*   *vote* → *voted*

3 When a verb ends in a consonant + -**y**, the y changes to -**ied**:
   study → *studied*   *try* → *tried*

4 When a word ends with one vowel and one consonant (e.g. *stop*), we double the final consonant:
   grab → *grabbed*   *plan* → *planned*
   stop → *stopped*
   But note that we do not double the consonant:
   • when it is **y**, **w**, or **x** (e.g. *enjoy*)
   allow → *allowed*   *enjoy* → *enjoyed*
   • when the final syllable is not stressed
   open → *opened*   *listen* → *listened*
   discover → *discovered*
   Note, however, that in Canadian English **l** is usually doubled, even if the syllable is unstressed (e.g. *travel*):
   cancel → *cancelled*   *travel* → *travelled*

* Consonants: b c d f g h j k l m n p q r s t v w x y z
  Vowels: a e i o u
  Syllables: |*hit*| = 1 syllable, |*vi*|*sit*| = 2 syllables,
   |*re*|*mem*|*ber*| = 3 syllables

Appendix 3: Irregular verbs

INFINITIVE	PAST TENSE	PAST/PASSIVE PARTICIPLE	INFINITIVE	PAST TENSE	PAST/PASSIVE PARTICIPLE
be	was/were	been	learn	learned	learned
beat	beat	beaten	leave	left	left
become	became	become	lend	lent	lent
begin	began	begun	let	let	let
blow	blew	blown	lose	lost	lost
break	broke	broken			
bring	brought	brought	make	made	made
build	built	built	mean	meant	meant
burn	burned	burned	meet	met	met
buy	bought	bought			
			pay	paid	paid
catch	caught	caught	put	put	put
choose	chose	chosen			
come	came	come	read	read	read
cost	cost	cost	ring	rang	rung
cut	cut	cut	run	ran	run
do	did	done	say	said	said
draw	drew	drawn	see	saw	seen
drink	drank	drunk	sell	sold	sold
drive	drove	driven	send	sent	sent
			show	showed	shown
eat	ate	eaten	shut	shut	shut
			sing	sang	sung
fall	fell	fallen	sit	sat	sat
feel	felt	felt	sleep	slept	slept
find	found	found	speak	spoke	spoken
fly	flew	flown	spend	spent	spent
forget	forgot	forgotten	stand	stood	stood
			steal	stole	stolen
get	got	got/gotten	sweep	swept	swept
give	gave	given	swim	swam	swum
go	went	gone			
grow	grew	grown	take	took	taken
			teach	taught	taught
have	had	had	tell	told	told
hear	heard	heard	think	thought	thought
hide	hid	hidden	throw	threw	thrown
hit	hit	hit			
hold	held	held	understand	understood	understood
hurt	hurt	hurt			
			wake	woke	woken
keep	kept	kept	wear	wore	worn
know	knew	known	win	won	won
			write	wrote	written

Appendix 4: Adjectives and adverbs

1 Comparatives and superlatives

1 We form the comparative and superlative of short adjectives (adjectives with one syllable*) with -**er** and -**est**:

cheap	→	cheap**er**, the cheap**est**
long	→	long**er**, the long**est**
warm	→	warm**er**, the warm**est**

2 If the adjective ends in -**e**, we add **r** and **st**:

late	→	late**r**, the late**st**
nice	→	nice**r**, the nice**st**

3 When a one-syllable adjective ends with one vowel* and one consonant* (e.g. *big*), we double the final consonant:

big	→	big**ger**, the big**gest**
hot	→	hot**ter**, the hot**test**
wet	→	wet**ter**, the wet**test**

Note that we do not double **w**:

few	→	few**er**, the few**est**

4 We put **more/the most** before adjectives of two or more syllables:

beautiful	→	**more** beautiful, **the most** beautiful
expensive	→	**more** expensive, **the most** expensive
polluted	→	**more** polluted, **the most** polluted

5 When an adjective ends in a consonant + -**y** (e.g. *happy*), the **y** changes to -**ier** or -**iest**:

dirty	→	dirt**ier**, the dirt**iest**
easy	→	eas**ier**, the eas**iest**
happy	→	happ**ier**, the happ**iest**
lucky	→	luck**ier**, the luck**iest**

6 Some adjectives have irregular comparative and superlative forms:

good	→	**better, the best**
bad	→	**worse, the worst**
far	→	**farther, the farthest**
little	→	**less, the least**

7 Be careful to use **fewer** with plural nouns (e.g. *stores*), and **less** with uncountable nouns (e.g. *money*):

> There are **fewer stores** downtown than there used to be.
> John earns **less money** than Mary.

2 Adverbs

1 We form most adverbs by adding **ly** to an adjective:

polite	→	polite**ly**	quick →	quick**ly**
slow	→	slow**ly**		

2 When an adjective ends in a consonant + -**y**, the **y** changes to -**ily**:

easy	→	eas**ily**	happy →	happ**ily**
lucky	→	luck**ily**		

3 When an adjective ends in a consonant + -**le**, the **e** changes to -**y**:

probable	→	probabl**y**
remarkable	→	remarkabl**y**

4 Some adverbs are irregular:

good	→	**well**	fast →	**fast**
hard	→	**hard**	late →	**late**

---

* Consonants: b c d f g h j k l m n p q r s t v w x y z
Vowels: a e i o u
Syllables: |*hit*| = 1 syllable, |*vi*|*sit*| = 2 syllables, |*re*|*mem*|*ber*| = 3 syllables

Answer key

Pages 2–3

A
1 see
2 do not/don't like
3 do not/don't taste
4 rides
5 have
6 drinks
7 want

B
1 She loves her job.
2 She hates cold weather.
3 She likes reading.
4 She hates basketball.
5 She does not like mushrooms.
6 She loves learning languages.

C
1 Do you like sailing?
2 Do you play cards?
3 Does Ken live in Saskatchewan?
4 Do you have a car?
5 Does Ken play soccer?
6 Do you speak any foreign languages?
7 Does Ken have any children?
8 Do you like scary movies?
9 Does Ken exercise often?
10 Do you enjoy public speaking?
11 Do you live in an apartment?
12 Does Ken like travelling?

D
1 Does the volcano erupt often?
2 Does the bus stop in front of my hotel?
3 Do the tour guides speak English?
4 Does that restaurant require reservations?
5 Does the temperature ever get cooler?
6 Do the locals have a favourite bar?
7 Does this area become dangerous at night?

Pages 4–5

A
1 Are they making cookies?
2 Is your boss getting angry?
3 Am I playing well?
4 Is your brother leaving?
5 Are they singing in the concert?
6 Are we moving?
7 Is he skiing up north?
8 Is she visiting her cousin?
9 Are we having dinner with Scott?
10 Am I speaking clearly?

B
1 Are they speaking Japanese?
   No, they're speaking Korean.
2 Are you reading right now?
   Yes, I'm reading a great novel.
3 Is Shea running in this blizzard?
   No, he's napping on the couch.
4 Are you writing an email to Igor?
   Yes, I'm telling him about my vacation.
5 Is Claudia dancing at the festival today?
   No, she's working at the information booth.

C
1 ✗
2 ✓
3 ✓
4 ✗
5 ✓
6 ✓
7 ✗
8 ✓
9 ✗
10 ✗

D
1 Are you enjoying
2 I'm learning
3 I'm eating
4 you are meeting
5 are you making
6 is teaching
7 I'm looking
8 are you doing
9 are going
10 we're going
11 is playing

Pages 6–7

A
1 am looking, find
2 is painting
3 wants, have
4 am calling
5 is having/has
6 see
7 is trying
8 stops, is it driving
9 is inviting
10 look, are working

B
1 ✓
2 ✓
3 have
4 are
5 ✓
6 am taking
7 am learning
8 Do you like
9 ✓
10 wish

C
1 I smell something spicy. Dad must be making chili.
2 Wendy has an appointment this afternoon.
3 He is working late again because he has an important meeting to prepare for.
4 You are speaking very loudly right now. Is your hearing okay?
5 We are building a snowman. You should come and help us!
6 She walks to work every morning.
7 I am watching my favourite TV show right now.
8 The wind is blowing the leaves everywhere.

Pages 8–9

A
writed
loved ✓
bought ✓
eated
passed ✓
found ✓
falled
shooted
read ✓
ran ✓
swimmed
made ✓
cooked ✓
buyed
shaked
waked
drawed
bit ✓
readed
threw ✓
write
winned
shot ✓
throwed
fell ✓
runned

stealed
drew ✓
maked
swam ✓
won ✓
woke ✓
bitted
finded
shook ✓
stole ✓

B
1 made
2 saw, played
3 said, didn't hear
4 hit, said
5 called, talked
6 Did you read, started
7 ran, ate
8 Did you enjoy, played, won

C
1 When did Caroline finish university?
2 She went to a movie last night, but she didn't like it.
3 Did you visit Margaret last week?
4 Jeff started a new business last month, and he hired six employees.
5 I saw Ashad the other day, but I didn't recognize him.
6 Maddie felt sick yesterday, so she went to the doctor.

D
1 took
2 Did you go
3 came
4 did you visit
5 went
6 had
7 loved
8 did you like
9 enjoyed
10 took
11 did you arrive

Pages 10–11

A
1 The storm started while they were driving home.
2 I saw an accident while I was waiting for the bus.
3 Mary went to several concerts while she was staying in Calgary.
4 My father was cooking dinner when he burned his fingers.

5 The soldiers were preparing to leave when the bomb exploded.

B 1 made, was making, arrived, helped
2 designed, started, was working, died
3 escaped, were taking, caught, locked
4 were losing, won
5 sang, played, recorded, was preparing, shot
6 were coming, were hurrying, was standing, grabbed

C 1 did you do
2 you were reading
3 rang
4 were you doing
5 was drinking
6 drank
7 went
8 did you put
9 was raining

Pages 12–13

A 1 used to eat, he eats
2 used to drink, she drinks
3 eats, she used to eat
4 eats, she used to eat
5 Did Roberto use to eat
6 Did Adelfina use to eat
7 Did Pam use to drink
8 didn't use to eat
9 didn't use to eat
10 didn't use to drink

B 1 ✓
2 ✓
3 ✓
4 ~~Did Pamela used to go to the concert last night?~~
5 ✓
6 ~~Jean used to spend a lot of money on that new jacket he bought last week.~~
7 ~~Kate didn't use to come to school yesterday because she was sick.~~
8 ✓
9 ✓
10 ✓

C 1 Dan used to play the violin, but now he plays the guitar.
2 Anna used to be best friends with Angela, but now she's/she is best friends with Celia.
3 Marisa used to take dancing lessons, but now she takes skating lessons.
4 I used to buy CDs, but now I buy mp3s.
5 Sun and Pierre used to live in Montreal, but now they live in Quebec City.
6 David used to drive a Yaris, but now he drives a Jaguar.

Pages 14–15

A 1 We've visited every province and territory.
2 They've studied all weekend.
3 I haven't slept well this week.
4 They've gone to the city.
5 She hasn't seen that movie.
6 You've found a treasure.
7 Have you tried seal meat?
8 Has Sam met Julia?
9 Have we finished studying?
10 Have they been honest with each other?

B 1 taken
2 raised
3 paid
4 heard
5 seen
6 been
7 retired
8 decided
9 wanted
10 read
11 planned
12 bought
13 forgotten

C 1 ✓
2 Have you ever been to the opera?
3 ✓
4 Have you ever been married?
5 Have you ever been to Mexico?

D 1 No, I haven't/have not eaten breakfast this morning. OR Yes, I've/I have eaten breakfast this morning.
2 No I've/I have never been to the opera. OR Yes, I've/I have been to the opera.

3 No, I haven't/have not read the paper today. OR Yes, I've/I have read the paper today.
4 No I've/I have never been married. OR Yes, I've/I have been married.
5 No I've/I have never been to Mexico. OR Yes, I've/I have been to Mexico.

Pages 16–17

A 1 I went
2 Did you like
3 I enjoyed
4 did you do
5 I visited
6 Have you been
7 I've booked

B 1 haven't/have not seen
2 went
3 Did you enjoy
4 was
5 've/have never heard
6 've/have been
7 did you do
8 stayed
9 needed
10 Have you ever won
11 won
12 Did you meet
13 've/have been

C 1 started
2 built
3 went
4 pulled
5 have opened
6 opened
7 went
8 opened
9 began
10 have built

Pages 18–19

A 1 We've/We have sold much more than we expected.
2 How much money have you spent this week?
3 How many people has Junga invited to her party?
4 It's/It has been raining for hours.
5 They've/They have been drilling holes in the wall all morning.
6 How long have you been sitting here?

B 1 've/have been doing the dishes.
2 's/has peeled (OR 's/has been peeling)
3 've/have been mowing the lawn.
4 've/have been defrosting the fridge.
5 's/has swept
6 've/have been peeling onions
7 's/has cleaned them.
8 's/has defrosted it.

C 1 been standing, been waiting
2 had, broken
3 forgotten, been sitting, noticed

Pages 20–21

A 1 had never gone curling
2 had already run in five marathons
3 had never written a poem
4 had never appeared on TV
5 had already played tennis at the Rogers Cup four times
6 had already written two novels

B 1 When the firefighters arrived, we had already put the fire out.
2 When the manager came back, Jim had already finished the work.
3 When Philip called, I had already gone to bed.
4 When their children came home, Alice and Jack had already had lunch.
5 When his wife got home from work, Ian had already made dinner.
6 The thieves had already spent the money when the police caught them.

C 1 had just left.
2 had been to Yellowknife.
3 had made some sandwiches.
4 had met her in Charlottetown.
5 had ever been to Japan.

Pages 22–23

A
1. are you going to eat, I'll cook
2. I'm going to buy, are you going to get, I'm going to look, I'll come
3. I'm going to leave, I'll see
4. I'm going to call
5. I'm going to travel

B
1. a You look hot, I'll open a window.
2. e Thursday is no good for me, I'm afraid. I'm going to meet the new manager of our Tokyo office.
3. b Next year, we're going to enter the Japanese market.
4. c Thanks, I'll have an orange juice.
5. d Take a break. I'll do the photocopying.

C
1. Nothing much, but I'm going to start a new job soon.
2. Thanks, I'll have a sandwich.
3. I'm going to do some shopping tomorrow and I'm going to (OR I'll/will) go for a swim on Sunday.
4. She's going to sing, I'm afraid.
5. No, but I'm sure you'll enjoy it.
6. David is going to (OR 'll/will) give me a lift.

Pages 24–25

A
1. We'll ✓
2. I'm going to
3. I'm going to
4. he'll ✓
5. I'll
6. I'm going to
7. I'll ✓
8. He'll ✓
9. I'll ✓
10. You won't ✓

B
1. I'll/I will buy the tickets before I go to work.
2. As soon as Jacques arrives, we'll/we will have something to eat.
3. The play will start after the music stops.
4. He won't/will not stop until he finishes the job.
5. When John gets here, we'll/we will go to the beach.

C
1. 's/is going to buy, 's/is going to write
2. 's/is taking
3. 's/is going to clean
4. 's/is going to buy, 's/she is going
5. 's/is going to do
6. 's/is going to wash, 's/is meeting

Pages 26–27

A
1. she'd/she would go
2. she lived
3. he didn't/did not eat
4. he'd/he would have
5. she got
6. he wouldn't/would not smoke

B
1. they discovered oil in Ireland
2. scientists reversed global warming
3. teenagers stopped downloading movies
4. astronauts visited Mars

C
1. I had good/better eyesight.
2. I could speak Mandarin.
3. I had a degree.
4. I was eighteen.

D
1. were fewer cars
2. drove more slowly
3. would have more time for reading.
4. ate less candy.
5. more people travelled by public transit
6. had more time to cook, would eat less fast food.

Pages 28–29

A
1. If she had spoken French very well, she'd have/she would have applied for the job.
2. If her friend hadn't/had not called, she wouldn't/would not have heard about the teaching jobs.
3. If she hadn't/had not contacted the company, they wouldn't/would not have asked her to go for an interview.
4. If the interview had gone badly, the director wouldn't/ would not have offered Anita a job.
5. If Anita had known some Japanese, she'd have/she would have started immediately.
6. If she hadn't/had not been good at languages, she wouldn't/she would not have made rapid progress.

B
1. had (not) lost, would have called
2. had (not) broken, would have gone
3. would have made, had (not) forgotten

C
1. I'd/I had told the truth.
2. wishes he hadn't borrowed some money from his mother.
3. wishes she'd/she had got up early.
4. wishes he'd/he had gone to the party.
5. wish I'd/I had sent Betty a birthday card.
6. Fiona wishes she'd/she had helped her sister.
7. He wishes he hadn't shouted at the children.

Pages 30–31

A
1. gets
2. get
3. do
4. made
5. did
6. got
7. gets
8. make
9. make
10. made
11. getting
12. got

B
1. had/made
2. had
3. got
4. got
5. did
6. had
7. had/made
8. done
9. did
10. made/had
11. did

C
1. do
2. made
3. got
4. had
5. made
6. do
7. do

Pages 32–33

A
1. brought them up
2. crossed them out
3. hand it in
4. pick her up
5. put them away

B
1. look up to
2. gave out
3. put (you) through
4. going on
5. broke down
6. Keep off

C
1. looked (it) up
2. get off
3. run out of
4. find out
5. try on
6. take off
7. put (them) on
8. head out

D
1. up
2. in
3. in
4. up
5. down
6. off
7. off
8. out
9. off
10. up
11. around
12. up
13. in
14. out
15. off
16. on

Pages 34–35

A
1. tore it down
2. get it off
3. break it off
4. break it off

B
1. got away with
2. put up with
3. drop in
4. Hang on
5. sorted out

C
1. going on
2. stopped by/were stopping by
3. made (them) up
4. come about
5. cut down
6. let (him) out
7. stay in
8. give up
9. laid off
10. shut (the factory) down
11. face up to
12. do away with
13. put (something) in
14. take out
15. set up
16. took (it) over

Pages 36–37

A
1. must like
2. can't come
3. can't belong
4. can't live
5. must have
6. must remember
7. can't want
8. must spend

B
1. can't be, could be
2. can't be, could be
3. can't be, could be
4. can't be, could be
5. could be, can't be
6. must be Smith.

C
1. might go to Portugal
2. must cost a lot of money
3. may come this weekend
4. can't take much interest
5. must work long hours
6. might be at the gym, might also be at the mall

Pages 38–39

A
1. have to, don't have to
2. don't have to, must not
3. must not, don't have to
4. have to, have to

B
1. don't have to
2. must not
3. don't have to
4. must not
5. must not
6. don't have to
7. must not
8. don't have to
9. don't have to
10. must not

C
1. has
2. Does she
3. have to
4. she has
5. must
6. does she
7. must not

Pages 40–41

A
1. Does Fred need a ladder, he does
2. Do we need to go to the store, we don't
3. Does John need to leave before lunch, he doesn't
4. Do they need to check the train times, they do

B
1. We don't need a lot of red paper.
2. Marc-Andre doesn't need to get everything ready today.
3. Marina doesn't need to leave at six o'clock.
4. Ann doesn't need a new bag.

C
1. For math exams, students need to bring pens and pencils.
2. For hockey games, students don't need to bring helmets.
3. For geography exams, students don't need to bring paper.
4. For art exams, students need to bring brushes.
5. For badminton games, students don't need to bring birdies.
6. For hockey games, students need to bring skates.
7. For math exams, students don't need to bring erasers.
8. For geography exams, students need to bring rulers and pencils.

D
1. didn't need to pay
2. didn't need to phone
3. didn't need to buy
4. didn't need to work
5. didn't need to take

Pages 42–43

A
1. shouldn't move the person yourself, should call an ambulance
2. should give you a new cup
3. shouldn't let him eat so much, should encourage him to play sports
4. shouldn't touch anything, should leave everything where it is
5. shouldn't drive home in her car, should ask someone to take her
6. shouldn't borrow money

B
1. they'd/they had better clean everything up
2. we'd/we had better take our umbrellas.
3. I'd/I had better go to bed early too.

C
1. ought to
2. shouldn't/should not
3. 'd/had better not
4. ought not to
5. 'd/had better

Pages 44–45

A
1. didn't/did not have to, had to
2. did you have to, had to
3. Did you have to, had to
4. did you have to, had to, didn't/did not have to
5. Did they have to, didn't/did not have to, had to

B
1. should have bought
2. shouldn't have gone
3. shouldn't have eaten
4. should have locked
5. shouldn't have borrowed

C
1. Colin had to work on Sunday.
2. Joanne didn't have to work on Sunday.
3. Derek should have worked on Sunday.
4. Marie didn't have to work on Saturday.
5. Brian should have worked on Saturday.
6. Daniel had to work on Saturday.
7. Joanne should have worked on Saturday.
8. Derek didn't have to work on Saturday.

Pages 46–47

A
1. are held
2. is spoken
3. was written
4. are checked
5. was built
6. are sold
7. were produced
8. was founded

B
1. are the Winter Olympics held?
2. is English spoken?
3. was "Hallelujah" written by?
4. are car speeds checked?
5. was the Ambassador Bridge built?
6. are souvenirs sold?
7. were the first Volkswagen Beetles produced?
8. was the *Montreal Gazette* founded?

C
1. The electric light bulb was invented by Thomas Edison.
2. The office was painted last week.
3. The accident was seen by several people.
4. Where are these TVs made?
5. The agreement was signed by six countries.
6. I was helped by a stranger.
7. The mail isn't/is not delivered on Sundays.

D
1. produced
2. were exported
3. started
4. were tested
5. was called
6. exported
7. are sold

Pages 48–49

A
1. was Mary examined (by the doctor)?
2. will the food be prepared?
3. has this window been broken?

B
1. was not examined (by the doctor) this morning.
2. will not be prepared on Friday.
3. has not been broken three times.

C
1. are made
2. was being built
3. must be finished
4. have been cleaned
5. were broken
6. has been stolen

D
1. has been won by the French team.
2. were being trained by a woman.
3. can be played by people of all ages.
4. was being watched by a large crowd.
5. was sent by the prime minister.
6. have been marked by two different teachers.
7. is being followed by a police car.

E
1. were built
2. be finished
3. been attacked
4. been made
5. be sent
6. be made
7. were being loaded
8. be delivered

Pages 50–51

A
1. has her food delivered.
2. had the/his meat cut
3. has her hair cut
4. had his eyes checked.
5. will have her blood pressure checked.
6. had her car serviced.
7. are going to have the roof fixed

B
1. They have their carpets cleaned there.
2. I must have the tires on my car checked.
3. I ought to have a new key made for the front door.
4. I don't think I can afford to have our apartment painted.
5. I had my watch fixed there last week.
6. My husband had his eyes tested there last winter.
7. have that coffee stain removed.

C
1. had his driver's licence taken away by the police.
2. had her bike stolen from the garage.
3. Fiona had her glasses broken.
4. John had his clothes torn in a fight.
5. Jane had her apartment robbed on the weekend.
6. We had our electricity cut off because we had forgotten to pay the bill.

Pages 52–53

A
1. to go
2. playing
3. to buy
4. to take
5. repairing
6. to visit
7. talking
8. to help
9. to pay
10. to live
11. talking

B
1. gave up studying
2. enjoy doing
3. deserve to pass
4. refuses to listen
5. keep studying
6. offered to help
7. promised to study
8. want to talk

9. stop asking
10. dislike listening
11. seem to think
12. need to study
13. have to find

C
1. to buy
2. to open
3. meeting
4. to call
5. taking
6. washing
7. to finish
8. to feed
9. to invite

Pages 54–55

A
1. is an appliance for boiling water.
2. is an instrument for measuring temperature.
3. is an appliance for cleaning carpets.
4. is an appliance for keeping food cold.
5. is an instrument for seeing things at a distance.
6. is an instrument for measuring speed.
7. is an appliance for keeping food frozen.
8. is a tool for making holes.

B
1. A: What does Khalid want the money for?
   B: He wants the money for a train ticket.
2. A: What does Philip want the flour for?
   B: He wants the flour for a cake.
3. A: What did Bill go to the butcher's for?
   B: He went to the butcher's for some sausages.
4. A: What does Helen want the polish for?
   B: She wants it for her shoes.
5. A: What did Alison go to the library for?
   B: She went to the library for a book on India.
6. A: What did Jane call Ann for?
   B: She called Ann for some advice.

C
1. wants the money to buy a train ticket.
2. wants the flour to make a cake.

3. went to the butcher's to buy some sausages.
4. wants the polish to clean her shoes.
5. went to the library to borrow a book.
6. called Ann to get some advice.

D
1. What did he come for?
2. A bus is for carrying passengers.
3. She went to the post office to buy some stamps.
4. The mayor came to give out the prizes.
5. The woman jumped into the river to save the child.
6. I'm training hard to get in shape.
7. This is a computer program for making three-dimensional drawings.
8. Can I use your pen to sign this letter?

Pages 56–57

A
1. Ann taught Jorge to drive last year.
2. Don't worry! Tomorrow I will persuade my father to see a doctor.
3. The boss has forbidden his staff to wear jeans in the office.
4. Last Sunday, Yan invited Sheila to come for lunch.
5. Next year the teacher will allow the students to use calculators during tests.

B
1. to come home early.
2. to work more quickly.
3. to do our best in the game.
4. to come to her party on Sunday.

C
1. she would like him to stay.
2. she did help him to finish.
3. he did advise him to stay in bed.
4. she does allow them to go to late-night parties.
5. she did remind him to call.

D
1. The driver let the elderly man travel on the bus without a ticket.
2. Jack made his younger brother wash the dishes.
3. I don't let people smoke in my house or my car!

E
1. watched Thomas make the sandwiches.
2. felt the ground shake.
3. see Brian leave early?

Pages 58–59

A
1. What's/What is Josiah like?
2. What are Angie's parents like?
3. What does Stuart look like? (OR What's/What is Stuart like?)
4. What does Katie look like? (OR What's/What is Katie like?)
5. What are Bob and Mike like?
6. What does Shannon look like? (OR What's/What is Shannon like?)

B
1. What does a double bass sound like?
2. What do kiwis smell like?
3. What do kiwis taste like?
4. What does a double bass look like?
5. What do kiwis feel like?

C
1. Who does your sister like?
2. What are Paul's brothers like?
3. What does Rachel like for breakfast?
4. Who are you like?
5. What's/What is Marie's husband like?

D
1. What's/What is Hudson's apartment like?
2. How was your boss yesterday?
3. What's/What is a squash racquet like? (OR What does a squash racquet look like?)
4. How's/How is your sister?
5. What's/What is Portugal like?

Pages 60–61

A
1. (that) she was going to a conference.
2. (that) he'd/he had lost his passport.
3. (that) they'd/they had been on holiday.
4. (that) she didn't understand.

B
1. (that) she was enjoying
2. (that) she'd/she had been
3. (that) she was
4. (that) she was staying
5. (that) they/her friends had
6. (that) she was leaving
7. (that) she couldn't speak
8. (that) she was going to take
9. (that) she'd/ she would teach

C
1. told
2. said
3. told
4. told
5. told
6. told
7. said
8. said
9. told
10. told, told

Pages 62–63

A
1. Jane to do the homework soon.
2. Ann to buy a map.
3. Mrs. Clark to see a doctor.
4. Bill to keep all the windows closed.
5. Paul to go home.

B
1. I reminded Frederique to call Sally.
2. The teacher told the children to wash their hands.
3. Paul asked Jessica to lend him her bicycle pump.
4. She warned the children to stay away from the water.
5. The policeman advised Maurice to see a lawyer.

C
1. Yes, and I told him not to be late.
2. Yes, and she warned her not to go outside the house.
3. Yes, and I told him not to forget the stamps.
4. Yes, and he told them not to go near the windows.
5. Yes, and she specifically warned me not to eat nuts.

D
1. warned them not to touch
2. advised her to take
3. reminded him to bring
4. ordered them to leave
5. asked him to come

Pages 64–65

A
1. if/whether.
2. Why?
3. how many.
4. if/whether.
5. if/whether.
6. What?
7. when.
8. why.
9. where.
10. if/whether.

B
1. Does Jim often play football?
   … Jim often played football.
2. What have the children eaten?
   … what the children had eaten.
3. Where is Mark going?
   … where Mark was going.
4. When is the next bus?
   … when the next bus was.
5. Has Ann seen this movie?
   … if/whether Ann had seen this movie.

C
1. if/whether he had worked since then
2. if/whether his sister gave him money
3. who else gave him money
4. if/whether he knew Steven Ellis
5. how long he had known him
6. if/whether he had seen Steven recently

Pages 66–67

A
1. a, –
2. –, –
3. a, the
4. –, a
5. an, –
6. a, a
7. –, an, the
8. a, –

B
1. –, the
2. the
3. a, the
4. –
5. –, –
6. a, the
7. –
8. –
9. –, the
10. the, the
11. the, the, the

C
1. an
2. a
3. –
4. the
5. a
6. a
7. –
8. a
9. the
10. a
11. the
12. –

D
1. a
2. the
3. a
4. the
5. the
6. a
7. a
8. the
9. the

Pages 68–69

A
1. There is, it is
2. There are, they are
3. There are, they are
4. There is, it is

B
1. There were five of us.
2. There were six of them.
3. There were twelve of us.

C
1. It rains a lot in April.
2. There's ice on the highway this morning.
3. It's very cloudy in the mountains.
4. There's a lot of wind on the east coast.

D
1. there was
2. there will be
3. there used to be
4. there have been
5. There may be

E
1. takes about five minutes to cook
2. does it take to make, It takes a few minutes.
3. takes about three hours to bake
4. does it take to make, It takes about twenty minutes.
5. takes about an hour to make

Pages 70–71

A
1. such
2. so
3. such
4. so
5. such
6. such
7. so
8. so

B
1. such
2. such an
3. such a
4. such
5. such a
6. such an

C
1. He's such a wonderful cook.
2. Those people are making so much noise.
3. He was/is so lucky.
4. She wears such pretty clothes.
5. They were so delicious.
6. It's such an unhealthy habit.
7. It was so easy.

D
1. so slowly that she didn't finish the exam.
2. so expensive that we didn't buy it.
3. so tired that he didn't go out.
4. so small that Oscar couldn't see them.
5. so much food that I couldn't finish it.

Pages 72–73

A
1. for
2. of/about
3. with
4. by
5. of
6. in
7. of
8. with
9. at
10. of
11. with
12. in
13. at
14. of

B
1. A: Is their daughter good at school work?
   B: Yes, in fact she is brilliant at everything.

2 A: Why is Mr. Lafleur's dog afraid of him?
B: Because he is often cruel to it.
3 A: Is Jenny fond of classical music?
B: Yes, she is very interested in Bach, for example.
4 A: Are you pleased with Peter's exam results?
B: Yes, we are very proud of him.

C 1 famous for
2 busy
3 full of
4 good at
5 used to
6 interested in
7 sick of
8 worried about
9 no good
10 worth

Pages 74–75

A 1 She is definitely from Dog Creek.
2 The meal is nearly ready.
3 He even lent me some money.
4 She certainly works very hard.
5 There were only two tickets left.

B 1 Tickets for the game have almost sold out.
2 They probably won't win the Stanley Cup.
3 He scored two goals and he also assisted two goals.
4 They just didn't play well enough to win.
5 They nearly won but they were unlucky at the end.

C 1 are almost unbelievable
2 just doesn't create
3 aren't very good either
4 was only released
5 has certainly attracted
6 and she can also sing

D 1 have worked well all day.
2 swam in the lake after lunch.
3 snowed heavily during the night.
4 did my homework in my room before dinner.
5 played better last week.

Pages 76–77

A 1 ✓
2 under
3 behind
4 ✓
5 in
6 beside
7 on
8 ✓

B 1 on, in
2 at
3 in, at
4 on
5 on, in
6 at, in

C 1 into, to, to, out of, to
2 into, from, to, onto, off, off, out of

D 1 from
2 across
3 along
4 past
5 up
6 in front of
7 down
8 through
9 under

Pages 78–79

A 1 c
2 e
3 f
4 g
5 b
6 a

B 1 in
2 in
3 by
4 by, by, in
5 by

C 1 at once
2 For example
3 in charge
4 by mistake
5 At first
6 on vacation
7 forever

D 1 In
2 on
3 in
4 but
5 on

Pages 80–81

A 1 ~~that~~
2 ~~they~~
3 ✓
4 ✓
5 ~~it~~
6 ✓
7 ✓

B 1 … the person who makes …
2 ✓
3 ✓
4 … the bus that goes …
5 ✓
6 ✓
7 … anybody who plays …

C 1 which/that takes great photos
2 they lived in
3 who made good Caesars
4 they are paid
5 nobody else wanted
6 where we ran out of gas

D 1 you can take as a carry-on
2 that needs film
3 that covers all the Mediterranean islands
4 we bought in that used bookstore
5 that have just been re-soled
6 we can walk all day in
7 that go with the green dress
8 I knitted myself

Pages 82–83

A 1 The sun, which is really a star, is 150 million kilometres from the earth.
2 Pierre Trudeau, who died in 2000, was a very famous prime minister.
3 Charlie Chaplin, who was from a poor family, became a very rich man.
4 The 2010 Olympics were held in Vancouver, which is on the west coast.
5 We went to see the Big Nickel, which is in Sudbury.

B 1 Soccer, which first started in Britain, is now one of the most popular sports worldwide.
2 Brian Mulroney, who was the prime minister of Canada for nine years, studied political science in university.
3 Michelangelo, who lived until he was ninety, was one of Italy's greatest artists.
4 Bill Clinton, whose wife became Secretary of State, was elected president of the US in 1992.
5 The Nile, which runs through several countries, is the longest river in Africa.
6 Madonna, whose parents were born in Italy, is a popular singer.
7 Gandhi, who was born in 1869, was assassinated in 1948.
8 Elephants, which are found in Africa and India, are sometimes hunted for their ivory.
9 The Beatles, whose music is still popular, were probably the most famous pop group in the world.
10 Calgary, which is in Alberta, is famous for its annual rodeo.

C 1 whose
2 who
3 whose
4 which
5 which
6 who

Pages 84–85

A 1 for the children
2 for the best drawing
3 since Carolyn's a vegetarian
4 due to a problem with the brakes
5 for some ketchup
6 owing to the transit strike

B 1 insulting her
2 the fact that
3 hitting his sister
4 the fact that they were repairing
5 working
6 Debbie's in the bathroom
7 the fact that some trees have fallen
8 the moose to

C 1 for
2 Since
3 due to the fact that
4 for

5 because
6 owing to the fact that
7 Since
8 for
9 to
10 for
11 due to
12 owing to
13 for

Pages 86–87

A 1 it was dangerous
2 Despite/In spite of
3 however
4 the fact that
5 my job is interesting
6 However

B 1 while/although
2 Although/While
3 however
4 Despite
5 although/while/
   however
6 although/while
7 however
8 although/while

C 1 However
2 although
3 in spite of the fact that
4 though
5 despite

Pages 88–89

A 1 Vanessa was tired,
   so she went to bed.
2 I couldn't sleep
   because of the heat.
3 Jill doesn't eat apples
   because she doesn't
   like them.
4 The streets were
   crowded because
   there was a festival.
5 I'll give Jane a key to
   the house in case she
   gets home before me.

B 1 in case she's at home.
2 because I want to
   lose weight.
3 because his passport
   was expired.
4 so I'll take a book
   to read.
5 in case there is
   another power outage
   this weekend.
6 because his wife
   was sick.

C 1 Last week, my brother
   lent me $40 so that
   I could buy some
   new shoes.
2 Last month, the
   government passed
   new traffic laws so
   that fewer people
   would have accidents.

3 Our school has
   opened a new library
   so that we can have
   more books.
4 Ann always writes
   everything in her
   agenda so that she
   doesn't forget her
   appointments.
5 Last Friday, we left
   home early so that we
   could avoid the
   morning traffic.

D 1 that
2 ✓
3 ~~so~~ because
4 ✓, ~~for~~ to, ~~so~~

Pages 90–93 (Review test)

1 a 2
2 d 4
3 a 6
4 a 8
5 b 10
6 d 12
7 a 14
8 b 16
9 c 16
10 a 18
11 b 20
12 c 22
13 a 24
14 c 26
15 b 28
16 c 30

17 d 32
18 b 34
19 c 36
20 d 38
21 b 40
22 c 42
23 d 44
24 c 46
25 a 48
26 d 50
27 b 52
28 d 52
29 c 54
30 a 56
31 d 60
32 a 62
33 d 64
34 a 66
35 c 66
36 c 68
37 c 70
38 a 72
39 b 74
40 b 74
41 c 74
42 d 76
43 c 78
44 c 80
45 b 82
46 a 84
47 d 86
48 c 86
49 d 88

Index

a 66
   or no article 66
   or **the** 66
such a lot of 70
above 76
across 76
adjectives 97
   + preposition 72
   comparative 97
   superlative 97
adverbs 74, 97
   -ly ending 97
   of certainty 74
   of completeness 74
   of emphasis 74
   of manner 74
   of place 74
   of time 74
   position in sentence 74
advice 62
advise 62
almost 74
along 76
already 20
also 74
although 86
an 66
answers, short 38, 40
articles 66
as
   reason 84
ask 62, 64
at
   place 76
   speed 78
   time 78

be
   there + be 68
be going to
   or **will** 22, 24
because 88
because of 88
behind 76
beside 76
between 76

by
   by car/bike/bus 78
   by chance/accident/
     mistake 76
   by mail/email/phone 78

can't
   impossibility 36
case: in case 88
certainly 74
certainty
   adverbs 74
   must 36
comparative
   adjectives 97
conditionals 26, 28
could
   possibility 36

definitely 74
despite 86
do 30
   in questions 2
   in short answers 38
   in the Simple Present 2
does
   in questions 2
   in short answers 38
   in the Simple Present 2
don't have to 38
down 76
due to 84

either 74
even 74
except (for) 78

fact: the fact that 84
fewer 97
for
   and, since 16, 18
   for example/sale/ever 78
   purpose 54, 84
   reason 84
forbid 62
forget 52

from
   place 76
front: in front of 76
future 24
   be going to 22, 24
   Present Progressive 24
   will 22, 24

get 30
   get something done 50
going to see **be going to**

had: in Past Perfect 20
had better 42
had to . . . 44
have
   + noun 30
   Present Progressive 4
have something done 50
have to 38
   don't have to 38
how 58
How long? 18
How many? 18
How much? 18
however 86

impossibility 36
in 78
   phrases 78
   place 76
   transport 78
in case 88
in cash 78
in spite of 86
infinitive
   to + infinitive 52
-ing forms
   after a verb 52
   spelling 95
instead of 78
into 76
it 68

just
   simply 74

like
What ... like? 58
would like 52

make 30
many
so many 70
may
possibility 36
might 36
modal verbs 36, 38, 40, 42, 44
more
comparative adjective 97
most
superlative adjective 97
much
so much 70
must
certainty 36
necessity 38
must not 38

nearly 74
necessity 38
need 40
doesn't need 40
didn't need to 40
never 20
next to 76
nouns
plural 94
uncountable 94

off 76
on
on business/vacation/
a trip 78
on TV/the radio/the
internet 76
place 76
transportation 78
only 74
onto 76
orders 62
ought to 42
out of 76
outside 76
owing to 84

passive sentences 46, 48
passive voice 46, 48
past 76
past participles 95
in passive 48
irregular verbs 96
Past Perfect 20
passive 48
Past Progressive
or Simple Past 10
passive 48
persuade 62
phrasal verbs 32, 34
place
adverbs 74
prepositions 76
relative clauses 80
possibility 36
prepositions
after adjectives 72
of movement 76
of place 76
of time 78
phrases 78
Present Progressive 4
for the future 24
or Simple Present 6
passive 48
questions 4
Present Perfect 14, 16
or Present Perfect
Progressive 18
or Simple Past 16
passive 48
Present Perfect Progressive or
Present Perfect 18
probably 74
purpose 54, 84, 88

questions 58
Present Progressive 4
reported questions 64
Simple Present 2
What ... like? 58

reason 84, 88
reason 80
relative clauses 80, 82

remember 52
remind 62
reported speech 20, 60, 62, 64
advice 62
orders 62
questions 64
requests 62
say and tell 60, 62
requests 62
result 88

say 60
Second Conditional 26
short answers 38
should 42
should have ... 44
Simple Past 8, 95
and used to 12
irregular verbs 96
or Past Progressive 10
or Present Perfect 16
passive 46, 48
Simple Present 2
for the future 24
or Present Progressive 6
passive 46, 48
questions 2
regular verbs 95
since
and for 6, 18
reason 84
so
or such 70
result 88
so many 70
so much 70
so that 88
somewhere 80
such a lot of 70
such a/an 70
such or so 70
superlative
adjectives 97

tell 60, 62
that
in reported speech 60
relative pronoun 80
so that 88

the
  or no article 66
there is/are 68
they 68
think: Present Progressive 4
Third Conditional 28
though 86
through 76
time
  adverbial phrases 74
  it 68
  prepositions 78
to
  movement 76
  with infinitive 52
too 74
try 52

uncountable nouns 94
under 76
up 76
used to 12

verbs
  + -ing 52
  + to 52
  + object (+ to) +
    infinitive 56
  irregular verbs 96
  phrasal verbs 32, 34
  regular verbs 95

warn 62
way 80
weather 68
What ... like? 58

when
  in past tenses 20
  relative adverb 80
where
  relative adverb 80
which
  relative pronoun 80, 82
while
  contrast 86
who
  relative pronoun 80, 82
whom 80, 82
whose 82
why
  after reason 80
will
  or be going to 22, 24
word order
  adverbs 74
would like 52